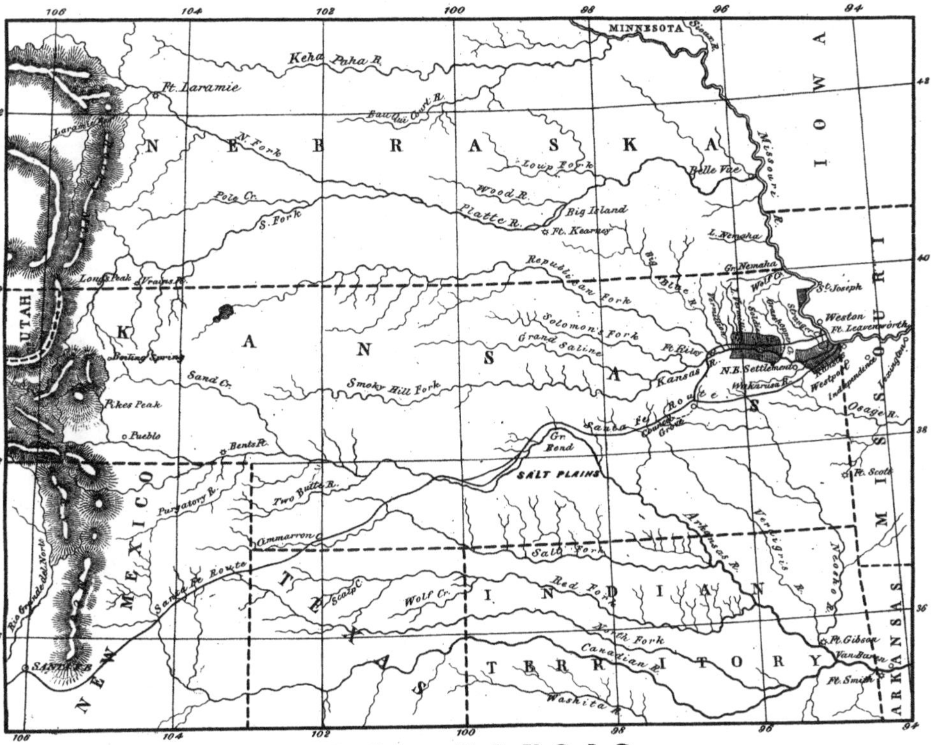

Middleton, Wallace & Co. Cin.

MAP of KANSAS
with portions of
NEBRASKA etc

Redrawn from official sources with emendations
by H.V. BOYNTON.

Moore, Wilstach, Keys & Co. Publishers, Cin.

A

JOURNEY THROUGH KANSAS;

WITH

SKETCHES OF NEBRASKA:

DESCRIBING

THE COUNTRY, CLIMATE, SOIL, MINERAL, MANUFACTURING, AND OTHER RESOURCES.

THE RESULTS OF A TOUR MADE IN THE AUTUMN OF 1854.

BY

REV. C. B. BOYNTON AND T. B. MASON,

COMMITTEE FROM THE "KANSAS LEAGUE," OF CINCINNATI.

With a New and Authentic Map, from Official Sources.

CINCINNATI:

MOORE, WILSTACH, KEYS & CO.,

NO. 25 WEST FOURTH STREET.

1855.

Stereotyped by
MOORE, WILSTACH, KEYS & OVEREND,
CINCINNATI.

COMMISSIONERS' PREFACE.

OUR first intention, after our return from Kansas, was to present only a brief formal report of the principal facts connected with the geography, soil, climate, productions, and resources of the country. But we soon found that the material we had collected was ample for a work of a different character; and it was the opinion of judicious persons with whom we consulted, that the interests of the cause would be best promoted by weaving this material into a cheap book of a somewhat popular caste, by which a wider circulation could be given to the facts themselves.

This course was decided upon, after consultation with the officers of the Societies by whom we were sent out, and the statements of the book have the official sanction of the Commissioners.

CHARLES B. BOYNTON,
T. B. MASON.

CINCINNATI, *October*, 1854.

PREFACE OF THE WRITER.

In September, 1854, a small party was commissioned by "The American Reform Tract and Book Society," and "The Kansas League," in Cincinnati, to explore and report upon the climate, soil, productions and general resources, and promise of Kansas.

With this party the writer united himself, partly for the purpose of aiding in executing the commission, and partly in the hope of recruiting his exhausted strength by a ramble over the "prairie land" of Kansas.

After the return of the party, it was thought that perhaps many of the scenes and incidents of that far, and almost unexplored Territory, which had so deeply interested us, might, through description, awaken an interest in others; and that the facts themselves, if conveyed partly through the medium of narrative, would make a more vivid impression, and obtain a wider circulation.

All facts and statements concerning the aspect, resources, and productions of the country, are presented with the sanction of the Commissioners; while, for the grouping of these facts, description, and narration, the writer alone is responsible.

CONTENTS.

CHAPTER VII.

CHAPTER VIII.

CHAPTER IX.

CHAPTER X.

CHAPTER XI.

CHAPTER XII.

CHAPTER XIII.

CHAPTER XIV

CHAPTER XV.

CHAPTER XVI.

CHAPTER XVII.

CHAPTER XVIII.

CHAPTER XIX.

CHAPTER XX.

CHAPTER XXI.

CHAPTER XXII.

CHAPTER XXIII.

CHAPTER XXV.

CHAPTER XXVI.

CHAPTER XXVII.

CHAPTER XXVIII.

JOURNEY THROUGH KANSAS.

CHAPTER I.

PREPARATIONS AND INQUIRIES.

Within the short space of a few weeks, a large amount of information has been collected and circulated in regard to Kansas. Every scrap concerning this last new land of promise, has been devoured with curiosity's keenest appetite, and most men will now talk *as if* Kansas were a familiar subject, studied and comprehended. Few, however, as yet, have formed any well-defined ideas of the position, aspect and resources of this great Territory, or have measured aright the influences which its settlement is likely to exert upon the destiny of the whole country; and two months since, when it was first determined that an exploring party should go out from Cincinnati, it was far more difficult to decide what was needed for such a journey than to provide an outfit for a voyage to Europe; and while we modestly admit that we had ourselves no knowledge to boast of, we must add, that the general ignorance was highly amusing. Some seemed to have no more definite notion of the position of Kansas, than of the distance of the fixed stars. They thought of it as indefinitely remote—somewhere "out west," toward the Pacific Ocean. One individual placed it two thousand miles from Council Bluffs; another brought it on within two thousand miles of Cincinnati, while an Irish friend inquired if it was indeed a newly-discovered continent. An outfit for Kansas is a matter to be very gravely considered, and attended to in the minutest manner, before starting, and a thing to be laughed over when once you are in the Territory. Rifles, shot-guns and revolvers, with all the necessary accouterments and ammunition, hunters' knives, blankets, tents, camp equipage, fishing apparatus, water-proof boots and coats; these, and innumerable smaller articles, were to be duly considered and decided upon.

Who could tell what weapons of offense or defense might be needed on the lonely prairie? All the newspapers agreed in declaring that no man should dare venture without his rifle, at the very least.

Whether the rifle was to be used against panthers, grizzly bears, and wolves, or against the Pawnees, or Camanches, or to defend ourselves against those bloody-minded members of the Platte County Self-defensive Association, who had offered a reward for Eli Thayer, we could not tell; or whether it mi ht not be necessary to carry by assault the famous Weston ferry, where it was said no Yankee could, on any terms, get over. A rifle was voted into the outfit; also, a "double barrel," for none could tell us how else food was to be obtained, and for the same reason our fishing-tackle was added, as also a revolver for close combat, whether with man or beast. Rubber overcoats and leggins were also obtained, for how could a shelter be reached on the naked prairie? We were told in the Territory, that a very prudent gentleman from New York, one of great forecast, had carried his precautionary measures so far, as to take out with him a paper of sand for scouring his knives. Our providence was not so far-reaching or so minute as his, but when fairly underway in Kansas, rolling easily in a two-horse carriage over the finest roads in the world, we discovered that our outfit, provided with so much anxious care, was, with a few exceptions, as little needed as it would be in the streets of our own city. Our rifle did indeed have a shot at a prairie wolf, and prairie chickens, quails and plover heard the voice of our "double barrel;" to which fact, most of them being yet alive, are ready to bear witness; while a few, impudent, and scornful, offering themselves at "*standing shot*" were added to our spoils, and we left their well-picked bones to bleach upon the prairies. The hunter's knife was quite useful, one morning, in preparing some dry toast for a breakfast on the prairie, but had no taste of the blood of buffaloes, or elk, or even grizzly bears.

In fact, the exploration of Kansas was a much more peaceful affair, with a more decidedly civilized aspect, than our friends had feared, or we had imagined. But, though bloodless, our journey was full of instruction upon points now intimately connected with American progress, interspersed with some exciting and many amusing incidents; while after leaving St. Louis, the whole scene was attractive, from its novelty, which scene, as it was a few weeks since, I will now endeavor to present to the reader.

CHAPTER II.

FROM CINCINNATI TO ST. LOUIS.

THE Ohio had shrunk, during the drouth, to a shallow that put to shame its boasting spring flood, and our Ohio and Mississippi Railroad being as yet only in "rapid progress," our party was compelled to set its face toward Chicago. But, by which route? This question suggests many important thoughts concerning the trade of Cincinnati. The traveler may pass by steamboat or railway to Madison, and thence northward by railroad to Indianapolis and Chicago; or, to Lawrenceburgh, either by the boat or cars, and thence to Chicago; or, by Hamilton, Richmond, and Indianapolis; or, lastly, by Dayton, Richmond, and Indianapolis. This assemblage of railways, stretching from Cincinnati toward the northwest, shows how earnestly she is now preparing herself to attract the trade of that immense and fertile region—while the long lines which traverse the country from the Mississippi eastward, some of them already crowded with freights and travel, and that leave the Queen City to the south on one side, cause one to feel that the air-line connection with St. Louis has been delayed too long already, and that it behooves Cincinnati not only to finish this railroad with all haste, but to be diligent and greatly in earnest to ally herself to the free west and northwest, by all those ties and living sympathies, which are mightier even than railways, to give direction to the currents of trade.

On one of the sunniest mornings of early autumn, we were seated in the cars of the Ohio and Mississippi Railroad. I felt the first motion of the train on this link of the great central "broad gauge" with strong emotion. Soon this broad gauge will stretch in almost an air-line, from St. Louis to New York; and already its westward continuation to the mouth of the Kansas is under-way, and then for the Pacific and the trade of the "exhaustless East." How soon, along this iron artery, the tide of commerce will throb from ocean to ocean! This spanning a continent with such a railway is a thought worthy the nineteenth century—one which no other century could have conceived or executed. It is an exponent of the spirit of our age, and marks the change in the direction of human thought and industry, since the time when the genius and labor of an empire were employed in piling up the good-for-nothing pyramids. Europe and Asia will yet rush to meet each other in this Western valley, at the rate of fifty miles an hour! At some eating station out in Kansas, or at Salt Lake, London and Canton will exchange congratulations and newspapers.

The sooner all idea of obtaining aid from the Government for building a Pacific Railroad is abandoned, the better, probably, and the sooner the work will be done. Not that it would not be a noble achievement for the Government, to link thus oceans and continents together, and make the commerce of the earth tributary to our own advancement, but the south, and the north, and the center, can never agree, as we have reason to fear, upon any route, and so let each section push its own lines westward as rapidly as possible. Each great division of the country needs a connection with the Pacific; and it is to be hoped that each will succeed in its efforts. In the meantime, the first and highest prize awaits the most energetic. A broad gauge air-line from New York, by Cincinnati, St. Louis, the Valley of the Kansas, and Fremont's newly-discovered Pass, need not despair of business. So at least I thought, as we swept down the bank of the Ohio.

The river seemed actually ashamed of itself, and tried to hide its shriveled dimensions, by creeping close up under the shadow of the steep banks, and winding, with its feeble channel, as much as possible, out of sight. I felt a pity for the old river that had held an exclusive monopoly of carriage here so long, and now, when old and feeble, was thrust aside, and made the theme of idle ridicule, by those who were once thankful to be borne on its full-flowing stream, kissing the high rim of either bank. The steam-horse snorted and neighed in derision as he rushed past, and the puny river had now no consolation, unless he thought of his fall-rise, and his spring-flood.

Chicago may be regarded as the most aspiring city in the Union, and certainly the marvelous progress of her youth, may well justify her in anticipating greatness in her maturity. It remains to be seen whether she is not stretching herself beyond her measure, and preparing for a calamitous reaction. She shows, as yet, however, no signs of weakness or pause, and though in every natural advantage she is far inferior to Cincinnati, yet there are powerful influences operating in her favor, which the Queen City does not enjoy.

The east has poured into Chicago and the adjacent country her sons and daughters, and capital in no stinted measure. She has followed these, of course, with her eyes and heart, her sympathies and prayers. Chicago has enjoyed, of late, whatever aid the influence of the east could give her. Toward her, the public attention has been turned; to her, capital has been directed for investment. The east has reproduced itself in that northern region, and the promising child is beloved, praised and recommended. In all this movement for the settlement and upbuilding of the northwest, Cincinnati is scarcely more thought of than New Orleans. The thought and sympathy of the east rolls along the lakes, and across to Iowa and Minesota, even to Oregon, and the memories and affections of these in turn, flow back eastward along the same lines, to New York and Boston, *carrying their commerce with them.* Chicago is the true heart of the country, of which she is the commercial center.

The rural population, the *people,* and the city, are in sympathy with each other. Their interests have thus become mutual, and they are rapidly concentrating upon Chicago an array of institutions and influences that will form a broad foundation of metropolitan power.

Chicago is an exponent of western sentiment as Cincinnati is not, and she is in closer sympathy with the general movement of the country. With these advantages, united with the unwearied energy which she displays, it perhaps were unwise to say, that she will not accomplish her large desires, inferior though she is to her southern neighbor, in position, size, architectural beauty, wealth and manufactures. Moral causes are entering largely into the control of commerce, and cities even, must beware how they violate the great principles of right.

St. Louis.—In studying the map of the United States, one involuntarily puts his finger upon the site of St. Louis, as the spot where the great internal city of the country *should* be, and feels compelled to prophesy, that there it must and will be. But here, again, moral causes interpose, and produce results, which, at first glance, would scarcely be anticipated. Slavery has repelled from St. Louis the element of freedom, and turned the tide of free emigration northward, leaving her own beautiful regions a waste, and herself languishing in an atmosphere lacking the vitality of freedom.

It is evident, however, to the most casual observer, that there is in St. Louis a new life contending with the old death-power of slavery. The young city, born of the influences of the surrounding free territory and its commerce, bears yet with her the body of that death; but the bands which lash the living to the dead, are loosening, and unless the Nebraska iniquity shall finally triumph, St. Louis will enter upon a new career, and the enjoyment of a better life.

Should Kansas and the States yet to be erected on the adjoining Territories, become slave States, St. Louis will command their commerce, as she will, also, the trade of the south, in far larger measure than she now does, excluding Cincinnati in large degree from both, notwithstanding all past and present efforts to secure the southern favor.

On the other hand, should those vast and fertile western regions teem with a free population, St. Louis, as a *free city,* will, in the end, interpose herself between them and Cincinnati; and then, if the latter is not allied to those frontier States, by any common sympathies or affinities—by any ties of kindred or the power of common memories and associations—if the recollections of their early struggles are connected only with other friends, will it not be difficult for her, in the absence of these things, to obtain the commerce of these rising States? Such are some of the moral influences which seem to connect themselves with the fortunes of western cities—and thus largely is the slavery question likely to influence their commerce and their growth.

CHAPTER III.

VOYAGE UP THE MISSOURI—CHOLERA ON THE BOAT.

It had been our intention to join the second party that went out under the auspices of the Emigrant Aid Society. This party, numbering about one hundred and thirty, reached St. Louis on Saturday, and instead of resting in St. Louis over the Sabbath, as we have since understood it was the intention of the officers of the Society that they should do, proceeded immediately up the river—thus trampling down one law of God, in a mission professedly undertaken to vindicate another.

This desecration of the Sabbath by a band of emigrants from Massachusetts, as most of them were, and connected as they were with a society organized for the very purpose of opposing an immorality, was a cause of grief to the best friends of the movement in the West. It served to divest the whole enterprise of a moral character; and to this extent diminished its power. Those who had denounced it, were encouraged in their opposition. The friends of the slave power had feared more than all else, that the spirit and principles of the Pilgrims would, by systematic effort, be planted in Kansas. But when they knew that this large company, the representatives, as they had reason to suppose, of those who were to follow, did not hesitate to prosecute their journey on the Sabbath, it served to modify, somewhat, in their minds, the effect of the religious speeches, and Bible presentation, and Pilgrim songs, that had heralded their approach. Their *Pilgrim* character was stripped away by their own hands, and they sank in public estimation to the level of a common band of adventurers. In a mere worldly point of view, it was a serious mistake, and it occasioned a loss of moral power not easily regained. It showed the necessity of a movement originating in deep and steady religious feeling, by which alone Kansas can be permanently secured for God and freedom.

To one unaccustomed to the navigation of western rivers, a voyage up the Missouri presents many novel, and some interesting, features. The union of the Mississippi and Missouri is conducted very much according to some of the modern ideas of marriage. The *two* do not become *one,* but remain two distinct and separate individuals, with equal rights and privileges, long after their destinies flow on together, between two common banks. Far below, however, it is perceived, that even the rivers find out that this is not the true philosophy of marriage, and they therefore melt into one. There are few such scenes on earth as the meeting of those giant floods, after each has swept over half the breadth of a continent, and almost half a continent still between them and the sea. We speak of them often, and of the great system of rivers, of which they form the central lines, as evincing the foresight of God, in regard to the commerce of the Western valley—as if they had been shaped exclusively for the trade of this nineteenth century. But what purpose were they subserving, in the economy of creation, through the ages during which they were all rolling on their floods before the Anglo-Saxons began to be? Even then they had some mission worthy of Him who unsealed their springs in the mountains, and scooped out their beds in the valleys. We are apt in our pride to imagine, that all the past has been shaped for our accommodation, and that by us all the future will be controlled. The veriest puddle of the streets need not blush beside the muddy Missouri; but one is deeply impressed with the *power* of the broad flood, that rushes down so unweariedly, with a velocity, as is said, of six miles an hour, nor slacking its speed in the race of two thousand miles, from the Rocky mountains to the Mississippi. It is a much more rapid stream than the Mississippi, and on the fortieth parallel of latitude, is said to be five hundred feet higher than that river.

Sand-bars are the vexations, and snags and sawyers the terrors of the navigation of the Missouri. Familiarity with difficulties and dangers, however, has begotten a coolness and skill, whereby they are avoided or overcome, and after watching for a day the maneuvers of a well-managed boat, among the snags, it is difficult to feel any anxiety about them, though reason gravely tells us there is continual danger, and she also tells the truth. Yet, compared with the whole amount of business, accidents have become somewhat rare, even on the Missouri.

These river steamboats may be said to be partly amphibious, from the manner in which they get out their legs and walk over the sand-bars and shallows. I once thought that when there is not water enough to float a boat, there is no remedy; but the western navigator halts not for lack of water. The boat is provided with heavy spars, some fifty feet long, which are set out over the sides, like the legs of giants, and by means of the proper machinery, worked by the capstan, the weight of the boat is partly suspended upon her legs, and she *literally* "*walks* the water like a thing of life."

The days occupied in our passage up the river, were among the hottest of the season, and the heat of the fires and steam converted the whole boat into one huge furnace, especially when not under-way. We knew that the cholera was doing a fatal, though quiet work, along our western rivers, as well as in the cities of the country, and even one whose courage is based upon Christian faith, could scarce avoid some unpleasant apprehensions, at the thought of the brutal neglect by which so many attacked with cholera upon steamboats, have been really murdered; nor should a man be called a coward, if his soul shrinks from a midnight burial at a woodyard, or from being hurriedly thrust into a hole in a sand-bar, from which the current may wash his body out before a day has passed.

Some symptoms of disease appeared among the passengers, though all was quiet. On the second day it was known to a few, that a young man who had left his wife and child in Illinois, to seek for them a new home in Kansas, was seized with cholera, and in a few hours more he was dead. The body was laid down on the guards of the boat below, away from the observation and knowledge of most of the passengers. The few who knew of it however, felt that they had received one of death's most solemn lessons, in this sudden vanishing of early manhood's dream—this swift fading of the temporal into the eternal, with one in our very midst, one of us—for among a company of passengers, traveling on for days together, there springs up a feeling akin to that produced by kindred, and a death on board resembles, though faintly, a death in a household.

What tidings, too, for the young wife, counting up the days of his absence, and consoling herself with thoughts of the new home on the prairie, that her husband was dead and buried, perchance where she could never find even his grave! In the night, at some woodyard, and unknown to all but the few who would bear the body ashore, he was to be buried; and perhaps it may interest the reader to know what reason one of the living has, to remember that night on a Missouri river steamboat.

Disease, which I well knew *might* be, and which I had much reason to believe really was, incipient cholera, had been upon me many hours previous to the sickness and death of him whom I have mentioned. My nervous system, from physical and mental exhaustion, was, before I left home, in a state to be *impressed* by every object, and by every occurrence; and doubtless the predisposition to disease, was strengthened by this solemn death, and the prospect of such a midnight burial; and, erelong, I knew that the disease was assuming its distinctive features, and that life's current had begun to ebb. A few moments' reflection brought me to two conclusions; first, that I had at my own disposal, as efficacious medicines as any one on board the boat could supply me with, and that I would depend upon them, my own judgment, and the overwatching care of God, and thus escape whatever danger there might be in making known a second case of cholera on board—for sometimes one's life is little cared for, in comparison with the reputation of the boat. Second, I knew that up to a certain point, even the aid of friends would be useless, and therefore determined not to disturb my traveling companions, unless it should be absolutely necessary. I sought my berth, with my medicines within reach, and committed myself into the hands of Him who I knew was able to save. The "practice" was necessarily a very simple one, confined entirely to the use of large quantities of powerful stimulants, frequently repeated. The boat was oppressively hot, but I knew that the perspiration that would gush from every pore, and then leave me all cold, was not caused merely by the heat of the cabin, and I was sensible also, that the system was gradually sinking; and, notwithstanding what I had swallowed already was quite sufficient to destroy a man in health, it was repeated, dose after dose, as the only hope, knowing that the fatal collapse was near. For what seemed a long time, I was not conscious of the slightest influence produced by these powerful remedies so lavishly applied; but as I now recall the visions and thoughts that hurried through my mind, it seems evident that the whole system must have been at last strongly excited, and there was, probably, a mingling of dreams with waking thoughts, a state of mind which, for a brief period, bordered upon, but yet was not, delirium. There was no fear of death, nor was there any higher exercise of Christian feeling than resignation to whatever the will of God might be. The mind seemed turned outward from itself, directed, probably, by surrounding circumstances.

About midnight, as it seemed, the boat was stopped, and I knew that the corpse of our fellow-passenger was borne ashore in the darkness, silently, with no kindred to mourn—with no funeral hymn or prayer; it was just at the time when I knew that my own fate would soon be decided, and that perhaps I, too, in a few hours more, would in like manner be taken away.

I followed the group with the body, in imagination, as I heard it leave the deck. I seemed to see the shallow grave hastily dug, the glimmer of the single light, the overhanging trees, and the surrounding darkness. Then the grave seemed to be only a hole scooped in the sand-bar, partly filled with water, into which the rude box, with the body, was thrust, and the wet sand scraped in, and I saw the current lay it bare, and then sweep it away. I thought of my own grave, under the cottonwoods of the Missouri bottoms, with nothing to distinguish the place, and I saw friends from home sadly wandering along the shore, and searching vainly for the spot. Then I seemed to feel that I was dead, and inclosed in a rough coffin, and buried in the sand, where I could hear the rush of the river washing my grave away.

Again, home, with every minute object of the familiar scene rose before me; the family rooms and circle of loved ones gathered there, and I saw brought in the letter with the ominous seal. I followed and traced the sensation produced by the tidings, in the larger circle of friends, and I remember a sense of sadness and mortification, when I marked how soon it was all forgot. I could not divest myself of the impression, that when I was dead and placed in my lonely grave, that there would be the agonizing sensation of being left behind, and alone in the darkness of the night and the tomb, that I should feel that the spot could never be found or known, and that I should hear the sound of departing footsteps, and of the receding boat.

When this partial dream or delirium passed, I was conscious at once that the progress of disease was arrested; the vital powers were beginning to rally; visions faded away, and I knew that God had interposed in my behalf. There was no doubt on my mind that the danger was nearly, if not entirely passed, and that, by the mercy of God, I had escaped a grave in the sand-banks of the Missouri.

The reaction of the system, so low had it sunk, was only to the point of health, notwithstanding the quantity and power of the stimulants, and my next night on the Missouri was one of comfort and peace. I had often read of the stopping of boats on these western rivers, at woodyards and sand-bars, to bury the dead; but now my own eye had seen, my own heart had been made to feel. One at least will not soon forget the dead emigrant, and that midnight burial. The banks of the Mississippi and Missouri are, in reality, one long graveyard, where the dead of all nations sleep, and their waters have swallowed up wealth enough for the purchase of an empire.

CHAPTER IV.

BUSINESS AND BOATS OF THE MISSOURI — KANSAS CITY.

Inasmuch as it has an important bearing upon the cheapness and comfort of emigration, the fact may be mentioned here, that we were agreeably disappointed at the amount of business, and business facilities, upon the Missouri. The number of steamboats on the river is greater, and they are larger and better provided, in every respect, than we had supposed would be found at this season of the year, while the amount of freight and number of passengers also exceeded our expectations. It shows a large population and business upon the upper Missouri, which fact is well illustrated by another. Weston, a place of some 4,000 inhabitants, is, by the river, 506 miles from St. Louis; and Platte county, of which this is the principal commercial town, has been settled only fifteen years, and now contains 40,000 inhabitants.

These facts show that Kansas borders upon a rich and populous country, upon which it can depend for supplies, during the process of settlement, whence it can derive abundance of stock, and where, also, it can find its markets, until it has commercial towns on the river of its own, and then it will have the power of choice. With such a country already settled, the Missouri river on its border, and markets within reach, Kansas will have advantages in its settlement which few new countries have ever possessed, and the settlers, consequently, will be exposed to fewer hardships and disadvantages. At this season of the year, (September,) and in this stage of water, (very low,) the voyage from St. Louis to the mouth of the Kansas river, is made in three and a half to four days, and the established price for cabin passage, on the best boats, is twelve dollars.

We were informed by the officers of our boat, that the Missouri was then at its lowest stage, yet this boat had very little difficulty in making her passage, though of 600 tons burden. The navigation can be depended upon until about the middle of November. It is then usually interrupted by ice, but is clear again early in March, and sometimes, in the latter part of February. The annual rise, from the melting of the snows in the Rocky mountains, occurs in May.

The price of freights, from St. Louis to the mouth of the Kansas, is, during the low water, from *one dollar* to *one dollar and fifty cents* per cwt., according to the character of the article, while, when the river is at full stage, and many Ohio river boats run up the Missouri, competition often brings it down to *twenty-five cents* per cwt.; and as the merchants of the towns up the river are able to avail themselves of these low prices, for the transportation of their permanent stock, the settler will often, perhaps generally, find it to his advantage to purchase his outfit of them rather than to buy at St. Louis, and then subject himself to heavy charges for freight — especially in the latter part of the season.

Friday evening, the Kansas passengers were informed that they must be prepared to land before midnight; but, unfortunately, it was found necessary to *walk* over a sand-bar, and Kansas City (in Missouri) was not reached until ten o'clock next morning.

City, is a somewhat ambitious title for the little village of Kansas, but it may be presumed to have a prospective import, referring rather to the possible than the actual. It is on the west bank of the Missouri, near the mouth of the Kansas, and on the southern shore of the latter stream. It appears like a village of from six hundred to one thousand inhabitants. Having a fine landing, with thirty feet of water, when the river is at its low stage; a natural limestone wharf, and a high bluff in the rear, it seems to occupy the natural site of the principal commercial city for the Kansas valley. Such it would doubtless be, were it not in a slave State. The line of Missouri, here, runs on the west bank of the Missouri river, close up to the mouth of the Kansas; and while the mouth of this river is wholly in Kansas, Kansas City is within the boundaries of Missouri.

What influence its location in a slave State may have upon its prosperity, remains yet to be seen. Prejudices which imbitter different sections against each other, while they are held apart, are often modified, or entirely removed, by mutual contact, business intercourse and social relations, and it would not be surprising if slaveholders and abolitionists should yet unite their interests and efforts, in building up a real city, where, as yet, there is little but the name.

In fact, Kansas City is already largely under the influence of eastern capital, and the wealth, and industry, and skill of the east, will be welcomed in every town on the Missouri.

Kansas City is already contending with Weston for the emigrant trade, as well as for that of Santa Fé and California, and should this latter place find the current of eastern trade and travel turned wholly aside from her doors, it will only prove what great and lasting mischief may be wrought, in an hour of folly, by a few noisy busybodies, whose self-conceit is much more conspicuous than their wisdom.

On the wharf, at Kansas City, long trains were preparing to start for Santa Fé, to us a novel sight, and giving us a more distinct idea of the extent of this southwestern trade. It was an American caravan, preparing to cross the American desert. The heavy, capacious black wagons are more worthy of the name of "desert ship," than the camel, for they are of a tonnage almost equal to a small canal-boat, and though drawn by humble mule-power, they make their voyages with great regularity. The manner in which the mules were hampered, previous to their being confined in the teams, appeared very ingenious. It was effected by lashing the head of one mule to the tail of another. It was such a meeting of extremes as we had not before seen, but the result was very satisfactory, and it would be an interesting question for some juvenile debating society, whether, in such a case, the tails were drawing the heads, or the heads were pushing on the tails. They all seemed to cherish a meek and quiet spirit, and marched in single file, with as much precision as soldiers on drill.

Just outside of the "city limits," Kansas river empties into the Missouri. It was now low, but with full banks, it is about three hundred yards wide. By the side of the Missouri, its waters appeared clear, and a calm beauty rested upon its smooth surface, as it seemed to lie asleep in the shadow of its woods. On its north bank is the Wyandotte reservation, where the land rises with a fine slope, from both rivers, and forms a beautiful site for a town, superior to that of Kansas City, in all except the depth of water at the shore, and facilities for approach. Here *may be* a rival city, on a free soil; and if so, the result is easily foreseen.

CHAPTER V.

A SQUATTER CITY — FORT LEAVENWORTH — WESTON.

About thirty miles above the mouth of the Kansas, we came in sight of an entirely new object, unknown to all former experience—a "Squatter City"—Leavenworth City, three and a half miles below Fort Leavenworth, on the west bank of the Missouri.

In spite of the President, and Cabinet, and treaties, the city has "squatted" upon lands of the Delawares, over which General Cushing has declared squatter sovereignty has no jurisdiction. Twelve hundred and more "sovereigns" have already, it is said, set up their thrones on these Delaware lands; and how they are to be despoiled of their kingdoms, is a question which the Government will not readily solve.

A squatter city has little resemblance to any other city; it belongs to a distinct genus of cities. This is a large and important one, the capital, as many hope, of Kansas, and is therefore worthy of description. There was one steam-engine, "naked as when it was born," but at work, sawing out its clothes. There were four tents, all on one street, a barrel of water or whisky under a tree, and a pot, on a pole over a fire. Under a tree, a type-sticker had his case before him, and was at work on the first number of the new paper, and within a *frame*, without a board on side or roof, was the editor's desk and sanctum. When we returned from the Territory to Weston, we saw the "notice," stating that the editor had removed his office from under the elm tree, to the corner of "Broadway and the levee." This Broadway was, at that time, much broader than the streets of old Babylon ; for, with the exception of the "fort," there was, probably, not a house on either side, for thirty miles.

Capital, skill, the spirit of speculation, and government patronage can accomplish many things, but to bring the trade of the Kansas valley up to Leavenworth City, would be a feat scarcely less remarkable than that of inducing the river itself to take that upward direction.

Fort Leavenworth has a situation of great beauty, on a rolling bluff, where scattering forest trees give it the appearance of a cultivated park. As a military depot it has importance, in connection with more eastern stations, but, as a "fort," it makes a meager show. From the character of the buildings in general, one would not suppose Uncle Sam to be the gentleman of wealth he is. But his means are principally expended for the benefit of his southern farms; and he is also reserving his funds for larger additions in that direction. Some of his western frontier possessions, on this account, look as if they belonged to a non-resident proprietor. To this remark Fort Riley forms a bright exception.

We reached Weston, a town of about four thousand inhabitants, in Missouri, on the east side of the river, three and a half miles north of Fort Leavenworth, on Saturday.

This place is the head-quarters of the "Platte County

Self-defensive Association, which is composed of a number of enthusiastic patriots, who have entered into solemn league and covenant to protect the Patriarchal Institution from the Abolition hordes which are hovering, like a cloud, on the borders of southern civilization, and preparing, by the introduction of Christianity and liberty, to put an end to the progress of the human race. Platte county has set its face like a flint, against the introduction of such fatal novelties as liberty for all—education for all—and the free use of the Word of God! At Weston was enacted the silly, but very expensive farce, of offering two hundred dollars reward for Eli Thayer. That advertisement will cost Weston, in the loss of commerce, more thousands of dollars than there were mills offered for Mr. Thayer. There are, in Platte county, a few precious drops of the very essence of slavery, undiluted either with humanity or common sense; and this advertisement is a fair expression of its spirit and its wisdom.

Neither the advertisement, however, nor the resolutions of this Association, express the sentiments of the people of Weston, whose business they have injured. They originated with a very small, blustering clique of lawyers and politicians, who desired a little notoriety, and who were supported, to some extent, by the slaveholders in the county adjacent.

But the business men of Weston soon saw that such a course would ruin the commerce of their town, and would drive from them a profitable eastern trade, which they are anxious to secure. This produced a speedy reaction, and the following circular, signed by one hundred and seventy citizens of Weston, shows into what contempt the "Fire-eaters," have brought themselves, and how surely the commercial interests of the river towns will compel a liberal policy in regard to the settlers of Kansas, and in general toward the whole east.

"CITIZENS' MEETING.

"*Weston, September* 1, 1854.

"At a meeting of the citizens of Weston and vicinity, G. W. Gist was called to the Chair, and Jos. B. Evans appointed Secretary. On motion of W. S. Murphy, Mr. J. B. Wright was called on to explain the object of the meeting. Mr. Wright addressed the meeting in an eloquent and able manner.

"On motion of G. T. Hulse, a Committee was appointed to draft resolutions expressive of the sentiment of the meeting. The following persons were selected: Geo. T. Hulse, J. V. Parrot, Ben. Wood, E. Cody, Col. Railey, W. S. Murphy and A. B. Hathaway. Said committee retired, and after a short absence, reported the following resolutions, which were adopted by acclamation:

"WHEREAS, *Our rights and privileges*, as citizens of Weston, Platte county, Mo., have been *disregarded*, *infringed upon*, and grievously *violated* within the last few weeks, by certain members of the 'Platte County Self-Defensive Association;" and whereas, the domestic *quiet* of our families, the sacred *honor* of our sons and daughters, the *safety* of our property, the *security* of our living and persons, the 'good name' our fathers left us, the 'good name' of us all—and the city of our adoption— and each and *all disrespected*, and *vilely aspersed*, and *contemptuously* threatened with *mob-violence;* wherefore, it is *imperatively demanded*, that *we*, in mass-meeting assembled, on this, the first day of September, A. D. 1854, do make *prompt*, *honorable*, *effective* and *immediate defense* of our *rights* and *privileges* as citizens of this glorious Union. Therefore,

"*Resolved*, 1, That *we* whose names are hereunto affixed, are order-loving and law-abiding citizens.

"*Resolved*, 2, That *we* are Union men. We love the south much, but we love the Union better. Our motto is—the Union first, the Union second, and the Union forever.

"*Resolved*, 3, That we *disapprove* the Bayliss resolution as containing *nullification, disunion* and *disorganizing* sentiments.

"*Resolved*, 4, That *we* as consumers, invite and solicit our merchants to purchase their goods *wherever* it is most advantageous to the buyer and the consumer.

"*Resolved*, 5, That we hold every man as entitled to equal respect and confidence, until his conduct proves him unworthy of the same.

"*Resolved*, 6, That we understand the 'Douglass bill' as giving all the citizens of this Confederacy equal rights and equal immunities in the Territories of Kansas and Nebraska.

"*Resolved*, 7, That we are believers in the *dignity* of labor; it does not necessarily *detract* from the moral nor intellectual character of man.

"*Resolved*, 8, That we are competent to judge *who* shall be expelled from our community, and *who* shall make laws for our corporation.

"*Resolved*, 9, That *mere* suspicion is not a ground of guilt; mob-law can only be tolerated when all other law *fails*, and then, only on proof of guilt.

"*Resolved* 10*th, and lastly*, That certain members of the Platte County Self-Defensive Association have *proclaimed* and *advocated*, and *attempted* to *force* measures upon us, *contrary* to the *foregoing principles*, which measures we do solemnly *disavow*, and *disapprove*, and utterly *disclaim*, as being diametrically opposed to common and constitutional law, and as having greatly disturbed, and well-nigh destroyed the order, the peace, and the harmony of our families and community, and as being but too well calculated seriously to injure us, in our property and character, both at home and abroad. We will thus ever disavow and disclaim.

"On motion of Samuel J. Finch, it was

"*Resolved*, That both papers published in the city of Weston, be requested to publish the foregoing preamble and resolutions, and all papers throughout the States, friendly to law and order, are hereby requested to copy the same.

"J. B. Evans, *Sec'y*. G. W. GIST, *Chm'n*."

From St. Louis down to the smallest business town of the river, eastern settlers and eastern capital will be welcomed; and the same interests of commerce will just as surely throw their influence, ultimately, in favor of Kansas becoming a free State. Thus, while commerce helps to sustain slavery in the east, it will inevitably aid to check it in the west, and foster the interests of freedom.

There is not the least reason to fear any serious collision between eastern settlers and the citizens of Missouri and other slaveholding States. The western merchants desire the business which eastern men and capital will create, and those who are speculating in city lots, must equally desire the influx of capital and men.

Mutual interests will make mutual friends; and we may be thankful that the east and the extreme west are thus mingled in the providence of God, in a manner which may allay prejudice and bitterness on both sides. Kansas may yet prove the neutral ground where the seeds of good-will may be sown; where the beginnings of peace may be found, and where the South and West may come to a candid and friendly discussion of the whole subject of slavery.

The lands in the vicinity of Weston, Missouri, are among the most fertile and beautiful in the State; and we thought it well to visit them before crossing into Kansas, in order that we might have the means of comparing the Territory with the richest regions in the States. We accordingly rode back among the hemp-growing farms around Weston. This district is high and rolling, resembling, in its *general* features, the region of southern Ohio around Cincinnati; but the soil is a deep black vegetable mould, to the very hilltops, equal, and we could not but feel superior, in fertility, to the best portions of the Miami or Scioto valley: a finer country need not be desired, if heavy timber is not considered an objection. This timber consists, principally, of black walnut, elm, sugar-maple, and oak, with cottonwood in the bottoms. This country is divided from Kansas only by the Missouri river, and farms are worth from *twenty* to *fifty dollars* per acre, according to location and other circumstances which affect value. The later crops had all been injured by the drouth, but still every thing wore the aspect of luxuriance, and extensive apple and peach orchards, in vigorous health, showed how well adapted the climate is to the growing of fruit. Peaches were selling, in Weston, at fifty cents per bushel, of fair, but not choice varieties.

After this visit to the hemp-lands of Missouri, we felt ourselves prepared to form an intelligent opinion of Kansas, and having provided ourselves with two horses and a light California wagon, in which we could sleep, if necessary, we crossed the Missouri at the steam ferry, about two miles below Weston.

CHAPTER VI.

WESTON FERRY AND ITS SHIBBOLETH — ENTRANCE INTO THE TERRITORY.

On Tuesday morning, September 8, we reached that celebrated steam-ferry of Weston, where, as it was said, in the early part of the season, the inexorable Missouri Charon drove back every one that betrayed his Yankee origin by his pronunciation of the word *cow;* and he was sent home to wander on the benighted shores of the east, and to starve on the rocks of the Pilgrims. But the eastern flood has drowned out the Examining Committee, and they are vainly waiting for the "ebb that cometh not." There might be established at that ferry a very effectual, almost certain, test—if there was no oath, in the first two sentences uttered by a stranger, he might be turned back safely as not a native of those parts.

Shiftlessness is a most expressive word, and it conveys more accurately, than any other I know, the leading characteristic of life in a slaveholding region. There is an utter lack and helplessness, in regard to all those expedients which insure convenience and comfort, with which a northern man is so familiar. Every thing is accomplished with the rudest means and most inconvenient manner. The western steam ferry would not be tolerated, in any important position, in an eastern State, for a single day. It would not only be the laughing-stock of a community, but would be abated as a nuisance. The descent to the boat is at an angle of nearly forty-five degrees, though nothing hinders the formation of a safe and easy grade; and, after what we had previously seen, we were surprised that the negroes were not used to carry the horses and wagons on board on their shoulders, as the simplest of all methods.

Over an open space, between the landing and the guards of the boat, some loose boards were cast; and thus the perilous plunge into the boat must be made. Fortunately, neither our necks or the horses' legs were broken. Another heavy lumber-wagon was, however, overturned in the attempt. On the opposite side, where an industrious man, with a few hours' work, could make a comfortable road, teams are obliged to clamber almost perpendicularly up the sand-bank; and for such accommodations the State of Missouri allows the proprietor of the ferry, to take from the owner of a two-horse team *one dollar;* and if his statements are true, at least six thousand people have crossed this ferry in one direction, (*westward*) this season, already. This, however, includes the California emigrants.

The first hour spent in Kansas, served to make a lively impression in regard to its fertility. From the ferry to Fort Leavenworth, three and a half miles, our road lay along the Missouri bottom, where every description of vegetation seemed to be on the magnified scale. The timber, principally cottonwood, oak and elm, was remarkably fine, many of the trees five and six feet in diameter, and conspicuously tall. Everything indicated a soil of exceeding richness.

Such bottoms are, however, by no means peculiar to Kansas. They are a common feature along the whole line of the majestic Missouri. They are fertile as heart could wish, but considered unhealthy, and on that account, are, as yet, not extensively cultivated.

Fort Leavenworth is beautifully situated on the swelling river hills. By the politeness of Major Ogden, we received such information and instruction concerning our route to Fort Riley, as assured us of a more pleasant journey than we anticipated, and we are also under great obligations to Dr. Mills, for an abstract from his meteorological record, giving us the means of instituting an important comparison in reference to the climate of Kansas.

Fort Leavenworth is an important position, as being the principal point of departure, for troops and Government supplies of all kinds, for Santa Fé, Fort Riley, Fort Laramie and Kearney, and other western stations, and the number of horses, mules, oxen wagons, and the large amount of stores of all kinds, required in these operations, is an important item to be considered in the prospects of the future agriculturists of Kansas.

For the purpose of giving an idea of the extent of this trade, we will mention here, that while at Council Grove, two trains of wagons passed, drawn by one hundred and eighty pair of oxen, while as many more were driven which were unyoked—beside horses and mules. These had been out to New Mexico with Government stores.

CHAPTER VII.

GEOGRAPHICAL AND COMMERCIAL DIVISIONS.

KANSAS is separated into three geographical districts, which deserve a separate consideration, and it has, also, from the features of the country, commercial divisions, which are differently arranged. Geographically, there is an eastern district, lying along the river and State of Missouri; a western one, stretching along the eastern base of the Rocky mountains, and a central tract, whose width, boundaries and general character, are somewhat variously stated. It has been stated, that the eastern district is bounded westward by a clearly defined, though waving line, where the fertile agricultural region terminates abruptly, and the line of a sandy desert begins. It has also been said, that this dividing line between the desert and the eastern farming district, runs from eighty to one hundred and fifty miles only, west of the Missouri river. This may be nearly correct in regard to Nebraska, but it does not convey a correct idea of Kansas.

After having availed ourselves of all known sources of information, in addition to personal observation; after conversations with intelligent persons, who have passed over portions which we did not visit, we conclude, that what we have called the eastern district, does not end abruptly at the edge of a sandy desert, but that its western portion changes its character gradually, as the slope of the "Great Plateau" is ascended toward the sources of the streams, till at a distance of about two hundred and fifty miles from the Missouri, the river valleys are narrow, and the prairie between them is sandy and dry.

If asked to point out the western boundary of this agricultural region, we should draw a line whose average distance from the Missouri would be about two hundred and fifty miles, but bending westward, still beyond this, on the head waters of the Kansas. This is an opinion to be affirmed or corrected hereafter. We are, however, quite satisfied, that a good farming region extends much farther westward, in Kansas, than has been generally supposed, and that future investigation will very much reduce the dimensions of what has been called the American Desert. In confirmation of this opinion, the following quotation from Col. Fremont's Journal, by which it will appear that there is a fine country on the head streams of the Kansas, some three hundred miles from its mouth. The starting point, in this extract, is at Fort Riley, at the confluence of the Smoky Hill and Republican Forks, which form the Kansas. On the 14th July, it will be remarked, he was two hundred and sixty-five miles from the mouth of the Kansas; that he was traveling *westward,* and nine days after, the appearance of the country is described in the last paragraph. It was by no means a desert.

"We arrived, on July 8th, at the mouth of the Smoky Hill Fork, which is the principal southern branch of the Kansas, forming here, with the Republican or northern branch, the main Kansas river. For several days we continued to travel along the Republican, through a country beautifully watered with numerous streams, handsomely timbered; and rarely an incident occurred to vary the monotonous resemblance which one day on the prairies here bears to another, and which scarcely require a particular description. Now and then we caught a glimpse of a small herd of elk; and occasionally, a band of antelopes, whose curiosity sometimes brought them within rifle range, would circle round us, and then scour off into the prairies.

"The bottoms, which form the immediate valley of the main river, were generally about three miles wide, having a rich soil of black vegetable mould, and, for a prairie country, well interspersed with wood. The country was everywhere covered with a considerable variety of grasses, occasionally poor and thin, but far more frequently luxuriant and rich. We had been gradually and regularly ascending in our progress westward, and, on the evening of the 14th, when we encamped on a little creek in the valley of the Republican, two hundred and sixty-five miles by our traveling road from the mouth of the Kansas, we were at an elevation of one thousand five hundred and twenty feet.

"On the morning of the 16th, bearing a little out from the river, with a view of heading some of the numerous affluents, after a few hours' travel, over somewhat broken ground, we entered upon an extensive and high level prairie, on which we encamped, toward evening, at a little stream, where a single dry cottonwood afforded the necessary fuel for preparing supper.

"The country afforded us an excellent road, the route being generally over high and very level prairies, and we met with no other delay than being frequently obliged to bridge one of the numerous streams, which were well-timbered with ash, elm, cottonwood and a very large oak, the latter being occasionally five or six feet in diameter, with a spreading summit. *Sida coccinea* is very frequent in vermilion-colored patches on the high and low prairie, and I remarked that it has a very pleasant perfume. The wild sensitive plant (*schrankia angustata*) occurs frequently, generally on the dry prairies, in valleys of streams, and frequently on the broken prairie bank. I remark that the leaflets close instantly to a very light touch. *Amorpha* with the same *psoralea*, and a dwarf species of *lupinus*, are the characteristic plants.

"*June* 21. During the forenoon, we traveled up a branch of the creek on which we had encamped, in a broken country, where, however, the dividing ridges always afforded a good road. Plants were few; and with the short swards of the buffalo grass, which now prevailed everywhere, giving to the prairies a smooth and mossy appearance, were mingled frequent patches of a beautiful red grass (*aristida pallens*), which has made its appearance only within the last few days. We halted to noon at a solitary cottonwood, in a hollow, near which was killed the first buffalo—a fine bull.

"At noon, on the 23d, we descended into the valley of a principal fork of the Republican, a beautiful stream, with a dense border of wood, consisting principally of varieties of ash, forty feet wide and four feet deep. It was musical with the notes of many birds, which, from the vast expanse of silent prairie around, seemed all to have collected here. We continued, during the afternoon, our route along the river, which was populous with prairie-dogs (the bottoms being entirely occupied with their villages), and late in the evening, encamped on its banks. The prevailing timber is a blue-foliaged ash *(fraxinus,* near *F. Americana)* and ash-leaved maple. With these were *Fraxinus Americana,* cottonwood and long-leaved willow."

There is, doubtless, a central belt of land, both in Kansas and Nebraska, where little rain falls, from the fact, that the west winds are deprived of their moisture, by the mountain ranges on the west; while this tract itself lies west of the line reached by the winds that come northward, from the Gulf of Mexico. The plains, in this district, are destitute of timber, the soil is sandy and the buffalo grass alone covers the surface with a scanty verdure. This, however, is an exceedingly nutritious grass, and the same country which supports such multitudes of buffalo, elk, antelopes and deer, is equally capable of affording pasturage for the flocks and herds of civilized life. To the westward, and as the base of the Rocky mountains is approached, an elevated region is reached — the western New England, or American Switzerland, abounding in beautiful streams, timber, and fertile and sheltered valleys. Here fall the intercepted rains, which, but for the mountain walls, would travel eastward, and be precipitated upon the broad plains beyond.

The general character of this mountainous country is nearly the same both in Nebraska and Kansas, except that the valleys of the south are milder than those in the high northern latitudes of Nebraska. The following description, by Colonel Fremont, of the regions around the sources of the Platte, or Nebraska, would be equally correct if applied to the western districts of Kansas. He was traveling westward, toward the mountains and up the valley of the Nebraska.

"*June* 14. Our route lay along the foot of the mountain, over the long, low spurs which sloped gradually down to the river, forming the broad valley of the Platte. The country beautifully watered. In almost every hollow ran a clear, cool mountain stream; and, in the course of the morning, we crossed seventeen, several of them being large creeks, forty and fifty feet wide, with a swift current, and tolerably deep. These were variously wooded with groves of aspen and cottonwood, with willow, cherry, and other scrubby trees. Buffalo, antelope, and elk, were frequent during the day, and in their abundance the latter sometimes reminded us slightly of the Sacramento valley. The next day we continued our journey up the valley, the country presenting much the same appearance, except that the grass was more scanty on the ridges, over which was spread a scrubby growth of sage; but still the bottoms of the creeks were broad, and afforded good pasture ground. Our course in the afternoon brought us to the main Platte river (Nebraska), here a handsome stream, with a uniform breadth of seventy yards, except where widened by frequent islands. It was apparently deep, with a moderate current, and wooded with groves of large willow.

"The valley narrowed as we ascended, and presently degenerated into a gorge, through which the river passed as through a gate. We entered it, and found ourselves in the 'New Park,' a beautiful, circular valley of thirty miles' diameter, walled in all round with snowy mountains, rich with water and with grass, fringed with pine on the mountain sides below the line — and a paradise to all grazing animals. The Indian name for it signifies 'cow lodge,' of which our own may be considered a translation; the inclosure, the grass, the water, and the herds of buffalo roaming over it, naturally presenting the idea of a park. Its elevation above the sea is seven thousand seven hundred and twenty feet. From this elevated cove, and from the gorges of the surrounding mountains, and some lakes within their bosoms, the great Platte (Nebraska) river collects its first waters and assumes its first form; and certainly no river could ask a more beautiful origin. The 16th and 17th we continued through the park, and fell into a broad and excellent trail made by buffalo, where a wagon would pass with ease. In the course of the 17th we crossed the summit of the Rocky mountains, through a pass, which was one of the most beautiful we had ever seen. The trail led us among the aspens, through open grounds, richly covered with grass, and carried us over an elevation of about nine thousand feet above the level of the sea. Descending from the pass, we found ourselves again on the western waters, and halted to noon on the edge of another mountain-valley called the Old Park, in which is formed Grand river, one of the principal branches of the Colorado of California. The appearance of the country, in the Old Park, is interesting, though of a different character from the New: instead of being a comparative plain, it is more or less broken into hills, and surrounded by the high mountains, timbered on the lower parts with quaking asp and pines."

The conclusion then is, that a much larger proportion of

both Kansas and Nebraska, particularly the former, is susceptible of cultivation than has been supposed, and that Kansas possesses the elements of one of the largest and most powerful States in the Union. Very little, if any, of her Territory will remain a desert.

In comparing Kansas with other Territories, or the States, it must be remembered that, in her eastern division, there are from forty thousand to fifty thousand square miles, in all of which there are almost no waste lands. There are no barren mountains, no swamps or marshes, no lakes, and no rocky hills. It is one vast, undulating plateau, exceedingly fertile, and ready for the plow. How many States in the Union can boast of even forty thousand square miles, which will admit of being cultivated? Add to this her central pasture grounds and her New England regions on the west, making in all more than one hundred and twenty thousand square miles, and it will be seen that, with her coal and mineral resources in general, she has the elements of an empire State.

Of the commercial divisions of the Territory, and the course of its future commerce, no very accurate opinions can be formed at this early period, yet there are certain large features of the country, which, instead of being changed themselves, must give direction to lines of communication, and determine the location of towns.

The northern portion of Kansas, on the Nemaha river, and Wolf creek, and the tributary streams, is nearer to the Missouri than to the Kansas valley, and this district will therefore demand a commercial depot of its own, on the Missouri; and as the railroad now in process of construction, from Hannibal on the Mississippi, westward, terminates at St. Joseph, it would seem, that in Kansas, somewhere in the vicinity of St. Joseph, a large town would naturally be built.

West from the Missouri, at this point, the country is fertile, and, in general, supplied with timber, and well watered, to the neighborhood of Fort Kearney, including the head waters of the Big Blue and Vermilion.

Time alone can determine what direction may be given to the trade of the western portion of this district, and whether it will seek the Missouri direct, or the valley of the Kansas.

The second, and central district, is the valley of the Kansas, including the valleys of the Smoky Hill and Republican forks, which unite at Fort Riley, to form the Kansas.

The importance of this district, over the other two, will depend, we think, upon two questions: first, whether the route of the Pacific Railroad shall follow the valley of the Kansas. The main facts bearing upon this question are, that a road intended as a part of the Great Central Route, is already located, from St. Louis to the mouth of the Kansas, as its present western terminus, and this road is soon to be opened to Jefferson City, one hundred and thirty miles from the Kansas line. Col. Fremont is also engaged, at the present time, in determining the exact position of a Pass in the Rocky mountains, supposed to be in the very latitude of the mouth and valley of the Kansas. The powerful interests connected with the construction of a road over the Central Route, seem to render it certain, that it will be opened at an early date, and it seems equally certain, that it must follow the Kansas valley.

A second question affecting the importance of this central

or Kansas valley district is, whether the Kansas shall prove to be navigable, for such a portion of the year as to render it valuable as a commercial channel.

The river has not yet been thoroughly examined. It is, doubtless, navigable for from four weeks to six weeks in the spring, as far as Fort Riley, and boats for that period may run one hundred or one hundred and fifty miles further up the Smoky Hill fork. The appearance of the Kansas, at every point where we examined it, between Fort Riley and its mouth, produced at once the impression, that it must be navigable for boats drawing eighteen or twenty inches of water, in even its lowest stage. Such is the opinion of most with whom we conversed, who had given the subject attention, and so great is the confidence in this opinion, that, as we were informed by one of the owners of the Excel, the boat which went up to Fort Riley last summer, that several small boats will be put upon the Kansas next season. We crossed the Kansas about one hundred miles from its mouth, and found it about three hundred yards wide, with five feet water in the channel, and running with a strong current.

A thorough survey can alone determine the practicability of navigation through the summer, but we feel much confidence that the experiment will prove successful.

Should it so prove, or should the railroad be constructed along this valley, then this central district will offer advantages for settlement, superior, at least for the present, to either of the other two, and in this case, also, a large portion of the commerce of the first, or northern district, will be drawn southward, along the tributaries of the Kansas, to the towns on that river and the railroad.

The third district occupies the southern and southeastern portion of the Territory, and is drained by the head waters of the Osage and Neosho rivers. A ridge of high prairie, called in the language of the country a "*divide*," separates these waters from those which fall into the Kansas. This ridge we crossed in passing from Fort Riley to Council Grove, a distance of thirty to thirty-five miles, and found about fifteen miles of it stony, though with a dark, rich soil, and fitted only for pasturage. In descending from this ridge we came into a most beautiful region, with a fair supply of timber upon the head waters of the Neosho river, where is the well-known trading post, on the Santa Fê road, called Council Grove or Big Spring.

This southeastern district is traversed, in the vicinity of Council Grove, and eastward toward Fort Leavenworth, by numerous small streams, some at this time dry, or nearly so, running southeasterly and forming the Neosho and Osage rivers.

We are inclined to think that this district is milder in its climate than that of the other two, and so far as we could judge, is quite equal to either in the fertility of its soil. Here, by early planting, a good potato crop, and perhaps half a crop of corn were raised, notwithstanding the drouth. It has no navigable streams, and for increased commercial facilities, must depend upon a railway either to the Kansas or to the southwestern branch railway from St. Louis, which strikes Neosho at or near the southeastern corner of the Territory. By the Santa Fé road, from Council Grove to Kansas, at the mouth of the Kansas river, is about one hundred and thirty miles.

Through the southern portion of Kansas the Arkansas river flows from the Rocky mountains, to within about one hundred and forty miles of its eastern border—a distance of nearly five hundred miles. What is called the Big Bend is wholly within the Territory of Kansas.

Of this portion of the Territory we can not speak from personal observation. From the testimony of an intelligent gentleman of our acquaintance who has passed down the Arkansas valley, from a point nearly south of Council Grove, we are led to consider this district as equal in fertility and general advantages to any other section of the country.

The Arkansas is much the largest stream which flows through the Territory, and is supposed to be navigable above Fort Gibson, and within the limits of Kansas, except in seasons of low water. That portion of the Arkansas valley which lies in Kansas, is in the latitude of Southern Virginia, and the nature of its climate and the character of its productions, may be inferred from this fact. It is said to be well timbered, especially in its eastern division. This valley, we think, should be at once thoroughly explored, and the nature of its soil, climate and resources, accurately ascertained.

Should it answer the expectations we have been led to form, from description, it would offer great advantages to a large colony possessed of considerable capital.

CHAPTER VIII.

SCENERY AND INCIDENTS.

This completes a general or outline survey of the Territory of Kansas. We will now return to the starting point of our journey in the Territory, which was Fort Leavenworth, and enter somewhat into details, mingling with our statements so much of the incidents of our journey, as may serve to illustrate our general theme, and convey a vivid impression of the country. We had already passed through Indiana, from Lawrenceburgh by Indianapolis to Michigan City, and through Illinois from Chicago to Alton; and as we were about to enter again a prairie land, we supposed ourselves already acquainted with the *general* features of the country, and expected a journey wearisome from the monotony of its aspect, and its similarity to what had been already seen. But the first hour's ride over the prairies of Kansas, spread before us such a picture, varying every moment and beautiful in every change, as we had no previous conception of, and drew from us continued expressions of a delight that would not be suppressed. One can form no correct idea of the prairies of Kansas by a previous knowledge of those of Indiana and Illinois; and residents in Iowa add the same remark of theirs. How, without the majesty of mountains or lakes, or broad rivers, and with so few colors as here are seen, such an effect can be produced, is worthy the study of artists. It is a magnificent picture of God, that stirs irresistibly and inexplicably the soul of every beholder. Young and old, the educated and the unlearned, alike feel the influence of its spell, and each in his own language gives utterance to his delight and wonder, or stands breathless and mute. There are many scenes, in Kansas, that can scarcely be *remembered* even, without tears. The soul melts in the presence of the wonderful beauty of the workmanship of God.

With ocean and mountains, with lakes and rivers, hill and valley, we had been familiar; but here was an entirely new feature of the beauty of earth—a thing apart and peculiar, but equal to any in its power over the soul, whether to delight or awe. The Kansas prairies cannot be described—mere words cannot reproduce in another's mind the impression which the scene has made; but if a man sees them, he is moved, in spite of himself, and the moment he would speak of them to another, he feels the poverty of language—he finds no fitting words.

The view, from the bluffs above Fort Riley, at the confluence of the Republican and Smoky Hill forks, is one of the most beautiful valley scenes on which the eye ever rested; it reminded me of some of the celebrated views on the Connecticut, by none of which do I think it surpassed. Not a human dwelling, except an Indian wigwam, has been erected there, and yet it wore the aspect of a highly-cultivated country. The green meadows and pasture lands stretched away to the limit of vision—the scattered tufts or copses of timber resembled orchards or artificial groves, while the bluffs on either hand rose with outlines which, though bold, were so flowing and graceful that it was a pleasure to the eye to rest on them. Still, though accurate description is so difficult, it will doubtless be expected that we shall make some statements concerning the general aspect of the country. Its structure may be said to be governed by its streams, along which run, first, the level "*river bottoms,*" on which nearly the whole of the timber of the country is found. These are sometimes, though not generally, too low for cultivation. On the Kansas river they are often five or six miles broad, and in fertility they are probably not surpassed by any lands on the continent. To these "river bottoms" succeeds a second level, elevated, perhaps, ten or fifteen feet above the first; level also, and in appearance and fact, equally productive. Above these, and from seventy-five to one hundred feet above the river bed, lies the high rolling prairie, whose ever-varying character gives to the country its picturesque appearance.

These features do not, of course, present themselves at all points with the distinctness and regularity which we have mentioned. Sometimes the two lower levels are blended into one, and again the streams, in their windings, will sweep to the very base of the rolling bluffs. The high prairie forms the *general surface* of the country, and constitutes one vast undulating table-land, whose main slope is toward the east and southeast, while in its smaller divisions it presents every variety of exposure, yet every outline is a flowing one, rounded to the line of beauty. Conical mounds sometimes rise a hundred feet above the general level, with a formation as regular as if shaped by art. Some of these are visible at a distance of fifty miles or more, and are bold and impressive features of the landscape. Again, far in the distance the river bluffs appear like the walls of gigantic fortifications, with parapets and even towers, as if the vast amphitheater embraced in their long lines were guarded by watching armies. In some places the prairie sinks gently toward the river, with an easy slope several miles in breadth, exactly shaped for beautiful farms; while in the background, under the shelter of the bluff, is the very spot for pleasant residences.

Here the low hills sweep round enough for a single farm, and then they inclose sufficient for a little community. Whether a man desires a level farm, or with an eastern, western, northern, or southern exposure, he can be suited; and if he desires all these combined in one location, he need not despair of finding even that, without one harsh or abrupt feature in the whole scene.

We will make here but one remark, in reference to soil. In general, it appears to be a black vegetable mould, deepest and purest, of course, in the bottoms, but usually *black* on the highest prairie; there, however, it is mixed somewhat with sand, which not only improves it for cultivation, but renders it more capable, than the low lands, of enduring drouth. On some of the higher bluffs we observed that this vegetable soil was not more than twelve inches thick, with a sandy subsoil, and at such points the surface was sometimes strewn with pebbles. These, however, are exceptions, and even in such locations the color of the soil is black. In some districts this dark vegetable mould is mixed with yellow sand and clay, so as to form a chocolate-colored soil, called by some the "mulatto soil," much prized for its fertility.

OUR FIRST MEAL IN KANSAS.

Incidents of travel, and descriptions of men and things, so far as they have a proper place in the picture of the country, may not be without interest even in such a report. We had been informed of a settlement which we might expect to reach in season for dinner, on our first day of travel; and at mid-day we found ourselves descending from the high rolling prairie, toward the dark-green line of fine thrifty timber that fringed and concealed a small stream now almost destitute of water. The small rivulet, however, was clear and bright—a *living* stream—that gave good promise for the health of Kansas.

On the opposite side of the grove, called here "the timber," we discovered, first, a corn-field, then a log barn, then a blacksmith's shop, finally, a log cabin, which group, together, constituted "*the settlement;*" and this, as we afterward found, was larger, by the barn and blacksmith's shop, than many Kansas "*settlements.*"

The "settlement," was located on a level bottom, whose fertility seemed equal to man's utmost desire; but the corn-field was the only experiment at cultivation, and that the severe drouth had injured. We found that "entertainment could be provided for man and beast." The youngest member of our party had just levied a small contribution on a flock of quails, and they, with a chicken born and brought up in the "settlement," formed the basis of a dinner just suited to the appetites that had been sharpened by the prairie breeze.

Under the cool "*piazza*" of our log hotel, where as yet no dirty floor covered up the natural beauties of the rich soil, a remarkably intelligent colored woman spread the cloth. She was a slave, and the few slaves thus far brought into Kansas are, in general, like this woman, taken merely as house servants, while no slaveholder, so far as we could learn, has ventured to bring what they call their "*force*," that is, the field hands, into the Territory. She was cheerful, apparently, and with the sole charge of the household, even of the hotel bills and funds. There was but a single circumstance which interfered with the picture of a happy slave. Her husband was a free man, and she was surrounded by a family of bright, intelligent-looking children—a little group that neither father nor mother owned—that might at any moment be sold and driven off with the pigs and calves.

To suppose an intelligent and high-minded mother, for such she was, happy under such circumstances, is a libel on the human heart.

The cloth was very white, always a promise of good things to come. The cooking was satisfactory; the preserved strawberries and plums, both the produce of the country, were delicious—and a milkman of Cincinnati would have deemed it a perfect waste to have served up such milk, so capable of bearing almost any quantity of water. The chickens that were not excluded from our dining-room, appreciated, as we did, the good milk, and vigilantly watched, not always in vain, for a chance to dip their bills in the pan.

Sundry dogs, the terror of polecats, and opossums, and prairie wolves, stood round our chairs, and seemed to think us no gentlemen in appropriating so much good meat to ourselves.

The bill was moderate. The slave-woman, very appropriately, as we thought, inasmuch as the slave code makes no distinction between brutes and men, placed us and our horses all on the same footing, and charged twenty-five cents a-piece all round for men and horses.

A rainy afternoon followed, which did not much impede our progress over the beautiful prairie road. Contrary to our anticipations, the roads in the prairie do not soon become muddy, and they dry, moreover, rapidly, when the rain is over. Covered with rubber overcoats we could snap our fingers at the showers, and kept on our course without annoyance.

Quails and prairie chickens were frequently seen in the road, or started up by the very sides of our carriage; but as one of our horses had no military spirit whatever, and dreaded a gun as much as Falstaff's soldiers did, we could not shoot from the carriage, without a probable race over the prairies—and the birds guessed our intentions as soon as we stepped from the wagon. Just at sundown, far in the distance the figure of a horseman was just visible against the sky. Soon it was apparent that he was armed with a rifle, and then that he was an Indian and had planted himself directly by the road, and with his gun laid across his saddle was silently awaiting our approach. He moved not as we drew near, but his glittering eye was fixed steadily on us, and it was not without some satisfaction that we thought of our revolver, and rifle, and double-barreled gun, all lying at hand.

It required no great stretch of the imagination to make one suspect that he was bent on mischief. It was raining and growing dark, and for what fiendly purpose he was there, on the lone prairie, at that hour, and in such a position, was not readily seen.

When we had approached within about fifteen feet, and he was abreast of our carriage, he hailed us, in words which we could not understand. It sounded like a highwayman's challenge, though the expression of his countenance betokened no evil intention. Again and again he repeated his demand, of which we could make nothing. At last we understood "Chebok, chebok," and when he summoned all his English and added, "*give some,*" we found out that the poor fellow had been waiting all that time in the rain so patiently, in the hope of getting from us a quid of tobacco. It is doubtful whether he believed us, when by signs we endeavored to show him that none of us either chewed or smoked tobacco. He seemed, like the dogs at the table, to think us no gentlemen,

We met with many amusing circumstances, showing the passion of the Indians for tobacco, in which it is but fair to the red man to say, they are more than matched by the white man's appetite in that region, and, so far as we could observe, the Indians were not so filthy in its use as their civilized neighbors.

At Council Grove, the family with whom we were staying had gone out on the Sabbath, leaving us in charge of the house. The Kaws, to the number of fifteen hundred, were encamped near by, and companies of them through the day, sometimes to the number of fifty, were in and around the house.

One old veteran came up to us with his blandest smile, which was very winning, set off as it was, by his shaved head, all but the crest and scalping-lock, and daubings with red paint, and went through with a very expressive pantomime, though *what* it expressed we could not tell. But he gestured still more earnestly, and smiled still more sweetly, till it thrilled our very scalp locks, yet we comprehended not.

At last he drew from beneath his blanket a bunch of matches, and drawing one over his hands succeeded in conveying his idea. He wanted us to loan him a pipe with which to smoke. We signified that we had no such article. But he was not easily baffled. He showed us that we could go up into the private room of our host, and by unlocking or breaking open a closet there, we could find a pipe, and he manifested no great regard for us when we refused.

At another time we saw an Indian, splendidly dressed, coming over the prairie at a rapid gallop. He reminded us of many a picture of an oriental chief. His head-dress, a sort of turban, was scarlet, and his blanket, also, was bright red, and of some rich material. He was evidently one of rank—a Pottawatomie. His leggins and moccasins were highly ornamented, and as he came dashing toward us, he looked as if he might be commissioned to warn the white man from his paternal lands.

Alas, the romance all vanished when we found that he only wanted some "chebok."

FIRST NIGHT IN KANSAS.

Night had set in, a dark and rainy one, and we were yet out on the broad prairie, how far from any dwellings of men, we knew not, with the not very pleasing prospect, that once out of the road we should be lost for the night. We knew, also, that although we might perhaps follow the road on the prairie, it would be utterly impossible to thread its windings in the utter darkness of the "timber."

The announcement of a light ahead, was as welcome as "Land, ho!" to the weary and homesick sailor. We had reached "the town" of whose existence we had heard. A town is composed of two or more log-cabins. This had just the requisite number, two. We learned at once that one of these was full. At the other we gained admittance. For the benefit of those who have never seen a hotel in Kansas—who do not know what pioneer life is—who are not aware how a man can live without comforts, and be quite *comfortable,* if he has a contented mind, with very few even of the necessaries of life, we will give a brief description of the spot where we passed the first night in Kansas.

It was on the bank of a clear and beautiful stream, about eighty-five feet wide in its then *low* estate, and the land upon its banks seemed rich enough to support the laziest farmer that ever grew fat on the unctuous river bottoms. The rain had made the black loam somewhat tenacious, and the mud on the hotel floor was, in the judgment of charity, a little *shallower* than it was without. It was of course a log dwelling, and it consisted of two rooms. One was bar-room, sitting-room, dining-room and sleeping apartments, and the other was cooking and wash-rooms, warehouse, servants' rooms, and all other rooms needed for a hotel establishment. The owners and all the inmates were Southerners, and with true hospitality the door stood wide open, and so did one of the two windows, and so they remained *wide open* night and day during our stay. With the window it seemed quite a matter of necessity to be open, as it was merely a "hole in the wall," without even a sash. An old colored woman whom they called "Beckie," was sole queen of the household, and mistress of ceremonies. She and her cook-stove, and meal-bag and wash-tub, and innumerable other things all dwelt together in the "*other room.*" Beckie's last "*clarin up time*" had evidently been "long time ago," and yet before Beckie is condemned as no housekeeper, one should take a look at the place where, and means wherewith, she was expected to produce order and neatness. In fact, she seemed to feel that the state of things was a stain upon her reputation, and she declared privately that she had "only just come."

Beckie had a kind, warm heart, under a skin that was of pure Ethiopian blackness, and when at the supper-table the blessing of God was asked for our food, she said that she believed it was the "first blessing that had ever been asked in the Territory;" that she had not heard a blessing in eight years; that her old master was a member of a Baptist church, and at "*one time*" used to pray. Beckie expressed her sense of the value of freedom by saying that "she wouldn't be owned by any body for a *thousand dollars*," "she owned herself," and she thought "every body ought to own themselves." The supper-table, and a stove, and four beds, as one might suppose, would be regarded as a *set* of furniture for one not very large room. But these were only the main articles, the outlines, as it were, while the "filling in" included all articles used for hunting, for farm and stable-work, beside cross-cut saws, harness, saddles and mill-gearing. The roof was *plastered* or *ceiled,* whichever may be the most expressive word, with strips of cotton cloth, nailed over the rafters, which were rough poles, and on hoop-poles laid across beams overhead, the musquito netting was ingeniously hung.

This spot is presumed to be the site of a city yet unborn, and which at this time has only "cast its shadow before," in the shape of two log-cabins, and lots staked out, patiently waiting to be bought. Our fellow occupants of the hotel were the sovereign squatters on the site and had participated largely in a meeting where terrible resolutions had been passed, excluding all abolitionists from Kansas, and making it (on paper) a slave State. A doctor and a lawyer were in the group.

Now if the reader imagines that we were very uncomfortable, and unhappy in such a spot and scene, he is wide of the mark. These "terrible resolution" men were very companionable, and appeared far better in private than they did in the newspapers. They came from the region where a reward was offered for that agitating Yankee, Eli Thayer, and yet we felt that every hair of our head was safe.

The blessing of God was asked for our food—one of our friends produced a Bible, and we read, and knelt, and prayed together, and the abolitionists, and the "*fire-eaters,*" three Yankees, one Kentuckian, and two Missourians slept under the same roof in peace. It was prophetic, as we could not but hope, of what will yet take place, on a large scale, in Kansas.

Such is the present exterior of things, beneath which are found kind hearts, hospitality and intelligence. Such rude walls cover many noble souls in Kansas, the germs of a future State. On this very spot there will soon be a real town, whose populous streets will present the attractions and refinements of cultivated society.

CHAPTER IX.

CLIMATE AND PRODUCTIONS.

Kansas lies between the thirty-seventh and fortieth parallels of north latitude. Now if we follow these parallels eastward, and observe the country which they inclose, an idea may be obtained of the climate and productions of this Territory, which needs only to be varied in view of local causes. To this should be added the fact, that the mouth of the Kansas is about seven hundred feet above the level of the sea.

Following the boundaries of the Territory eastward to the Atlantic, we find its southern line passing through southern Missouri, central Kentucky, and southern Virginia. Its northern boundary runs through northern Missouri, central Illinois, central Indiana, southern Ohio, and southern Pennsylvania, striking the sea-coast in the latitude of Philadelphia.

Except as modified by its remoteness from the ocean, we should expect that Kansas would resemble these States in its climate and productions. Experience has shown that its soil is capable of producing, in perfection, all the grains, vegetables, and fruits which can be grown in the middle States. If, as is stated, the latter part of the summer is often dry, though seldom visited by such a drouth as has this season prevailed through the whole country, it would indicate the necessity of early planting and sowing; the advantages of which are, this season, shown by the fact that at Council Grove, early planted potatoes produced a good crop, and early planted corn also was not a failure.

The ground is usually free from frost in the latter part of February, or early in March, and the character of the soil admits of early plowing; earlier, it is said, than in the corresponding latitudes farther east. Fall planted potatoes might, perhaps, succeed best.

The first frosts occur about the 1st of October; but for two months later the prairies afford pasturage for stock, while young cattle, where they can be sheltered by the timber, are wintered with very little feeding — though abundance of food and warm shelters will be found, as elsewhere, to be needed for the most profitable stock-raising.

The meteorological records which were furnished us by the politeness of the officers at forts Leavenworth and Riley, show that but small quantities of rain fell in the Territory during the winters, and consequently that the roads, except for a small portion of the year, must be in good condition, and the weather suitable for outdoor work.

CHAPTER X.

TEMPERATURE AND QUANTITY OF RAIN.

THE range of the thermometer, in the winters of 1853-4, was as follows:

Fort Leavenworth, 9 o'clock, A. M.

1853.				1854.			
Jan.	1..17°	Feb.	1..43°	Jan.	1..31°	Feb.	1..44°
"	2..16	"	2..23	"	2..34	"	2..21
"	3.. 1	"	3..32	"	3..56	"	3..23
"	4..15	"	4.. 1	"	4..43	"	4..37
"	5..20	"	5.. 5	"	5.. 8	"	5..38
"	6..37	"	6..12	"	6.. 2	"	6..34
"	7..37	"	7..17	"	7..18	"	7..33
"	8..36	"	8.. 5	"	8..19	"	8..30
"	9..31	"	9..19	"	9..33	"	9..42
"	10..34	"	10..42	"	10..38	"	10..40
"	11..32	"	11..42	"	11..17	"	11..59
"	12..33	"	12..32	"	12..18	"	12..64
"	13..33	"	13..32	"	13.. 7	"	13..35
"	14..29	"	14..20	"	14..10	"	14..31
"	15..23	"	15..41	"	15..28	"	15..17
"	16..22	"	16..20	"	16.. 8	"	16..17
"	17..24	"	17..40	"	17..10	"	17..18
"	18..28	"	18..25	"	18..10	"	18..38
"	19..26	"	19..20	"	19..22	"	19..39
"	20..29	"	20..37	"	20.. 8	"	20..38

Jan. 21 . . 39°	Feb. 21 . . 41°	Jan. 21 . . 10°	Feb. 21 . . 37°
" 22 . . 22	" 22 . . 30	" 22 . . 0	" 22 . . 37
" 23 . . 45	" 23 . . 15	" 23 . . 6	" 23 . . 34
" 24 . . 33	" 24 . . 37	" 24 . . 14	" 24 . . 40
" 25 . . 33	" 25 . . 34	" 25 . . 40	" 25 . . 34
" 26 . . 10	" 26 . . 54	" 26 . . 28	" 26 . . 32
" 27 . . 36	" 27 . . 50	" 27 . . 20	" 27 . . 29
" 28 . . 37	" 28 . . 31	" 28 . . 40	" 28 . . 33
" 29 . . 42		" 29 . . 30	
" 30 . . 31		" 30 . . 57	
" 31 . . 32		" 31 . . 44	
28.41	25.07	22.06	34.78
Monthly Mean.	"	"	

Position of the Thermometer 160 feet above Missouri.

At Fort Riley, one hundred and forty miles west of Fort Leavenworth, the monthly mean for Jan. 1854, was 23° 59′, and for February '54, 37° 11′, showing that at the westernmost post the average temperature was a few degrees higher than on the Missouri river.

In the years which these records cover, the highest range of the thermometer was, at Fort Leavenworth 102°, and at Fort Riley 105°, during the last summer; and the lowest was at Fort Leavenworth, eight degrees below zero, and at Fort Riley, twelve degrees below zero.

A record of temperature kept while we were in the Territory, compared with one for the corresponding days at Cincinnati, shows no important difference; and the general conclusion is, that the climate of Kansas, in *temperature*, corresponds very nearly to that of southern Ohio, Kentucky, and Virginia; while from the data which we have been able to procure, the indications are that it is less variable.

Another important question concerns the annual quantity of rain which falls in Kansas.

The fact that the annual quantity of rain diminishes as we leave the coasts of continents for the interior, and that Kansas is nearly in the center of North America, would lead to the conclusion that it is a land of drought, unfit for agricultural purposes. Such indeed is the impression upon many minds; and we were informed while on our journey, that so little rain falls at Fort Riley and Council Grove, as to render the country nearly valueless. Fortunately, we have the means of a somewhat extended comparison, from which a perfectly reliable and scientific conclusion is reached.

QUANTITY OF RAIN AT DIFFERENT POINTS.

Fort Leavenworth, K. T., in 1853,	30	in. 45-100dths	perp.	depth.
Annual mean quant. Cam., Mass.,	38	"	"	"
Western Reserve College, Ohio,	36	"	"	"
Fort Crawford, Wisconsin, . .	30	"	"	"
Marietta, Ohio, ...	41	"	"	"
Philadelphia, Pennsylvania, . .	45	"	"	"
St. Louis, Missouri, ...	32	"	"	"
British Islands, ...	32	"	"	"
Western Franee, ...	25	"	"	"
Eastern France, ...	22	"	"	"
Central and North. Germany, .	20	"	"	"
Hungary, ...	17	"	"	"
Mean quantity for the Old World,	34	"	"	"
Mean quantity for America, . .	35	"	"	"

In this year of universal drought, we have not the means of a comparison, but at Fort Leavenworth, from January 1, 1854, to August 31, the quantity was 12 in. 49-100dths.

At Fort Riley, one hundred and forty miles west of Fort Leavenworth, the quantity, for the same period, was 15 in.; and at the same place, from November 1, 1853, to September 15, 1854, the quantity was 24 in. 86-100dths.

These facts, taken together, are quite sufficient to show that Kansas does not suffer from a deficiency of rain. In addition, it should be stated, that except in the river bottoms, the soil is of a character that renders it a vast reservoir of the water which falls. It sinks deep, and remains to supply the roots of plants when the surface is dry.

CHAPTER XI.

STREAMS, SPRINGS, WELLS, TIMBER—ITS KINDS AND QUANTITY—MATERIALS FOR FENCES AND DWELLINGS.

KANSAS may be regarded as a land of springs and streams. The larger rivers are the Nemaha and Wolf creek in the north; the Kansas, with its tributaries, occupying the central valley, and the Arkansas with the head waters of the Osage and Neosho in the south. A glance at the map shows that these cover all the eastern division of the Territory with a network of waters.

The head streams of the Kansas stretch far toward the Rocky mountains, while its main tributary on the north, the Big Blue, flows from within the limits of Nebraska.

The Arkansas runs for about five hundred miles within the limits of the Territory, and while a portion of its valley is represented as sandy, yet all the lower portion is said to be heavily timbered and fertile, while its mild climate will recommend it to a large class of settlers. It is by no means destitute of groves and fertile tracts of land, high up toward its sources, as is shown by the settlement at Pueblo, which is more than five hundred miles west of the mouth of the Kansas, and the State of Missouri.

The Neosho, the Marais De Cygnes, and the Osage in the

southeast, find their sources in the region of country around Council Grove, which in beauty and fertility can scarcely be surpassed.

We traveled through the country a distance of more than three hundred miles, and though many of the small streams and springs had become dry, as was the case in every other part of the country, yet we found no difficulty in obtaining water, at suitable intervals, for ourselves and horses, without leaving the main roads.

It is a land of springs, which indeed might be inferred from its undulating character, and living water may probably be found in nearly every section of land. It is probable that at some points wells must be depended on for the use of cattle, yet even this is questionable. The deepest well we saw had been sunk thirty-five feet, and the temperature of several which we tried was 54° Fahrenheit.

Some of these wells and springs supply water suitable for washing, but in general, we think, it is what is called "*hard.*"

Many good mill-sites are already known on the various streams, and some of them are occupied; but from the abundant indications of coal, it is probable, almost certain, that steam-power can be cheaply supplied, and will be chiefly employed for manufacturing purposes.

We saw no streams in the country, except the Kansas, whose waters are turbid. Even those of the Big Blue are clear, and beautiful, reminding one of the streams of New England. The rivers and streams of the Territory abound with fish.

Among the timber trees of the country, the following are

the chief: white oak, black oak, red oak, hickory, sugar-maple, red-flowering or soft-maple, poplar, cottonwood, elm, mucilaginous elm, sycamore, ash, black walnut, honey locust, black locust, linden, beech, wild cherry, hackberry and box elder. A few cedars were seen near the mouth of the Big Blue, and this tree is also found in the neighborhood of Fort Riley. The western district abounds with pines, and other timber belonging to a colder climate and mountain ranges.

In some locations on the north side of the Kansas, the timber is short, and has a scraggy, unthrifty appearance. In general, however, it seems not inferior to that of other sections of our country, and much of it has attained to a gigantic size.

Many of the oaks are five or six feet in diameter, and the cottonwood is frequently larger even than that. The timber at the junction of the Smoky Hill and Republican Forks, is remarkably fine, and where it is crossed by the Council Grove road, is more than two miles broad.

Enormous elms, oaks, cottonwoods, and sycamores stand thick on all the ground. At the steam-mill there were solid logs, showing a thrifty growth four and five feet in diameter, of oak and cottonwood. On the upper tributaries of the Osage and Neosho, around Council Grove, the timber appears remarkably thrifty, and shoots up to a great hight—and there also, the quantity appears sufficient to supply every want.

The general impression seems to be that the deficiency of timber is so great as to present a serious, if not insurmountable obstacle to the settlement of the country, and consequently each squatter has made it his first object to secure a tract of timber both indispensable for his own farm, and as a profitable investment, from the opinion that timber and fuel must be both scarce and dear.

This subject is one of prime importance, and deserves a careful consideration; for if prairie farms, destitute of timber, can not be cultivated successfully, then, except for stock-raising, Kansas will prove of but little value. If the prairie farmer is to be at the mercy of the owner of timber, and *tree-tops*, for fuel, are to be sold at five dollars per cord, as in some locations now, it will be long before the Territory is changed into a populous State.

We incline to the opinion, however, that little difficulty need be apprehended from this cause, with judicious management. First of all, there is more timber in Kansas than meets the eye of one passing through the country. It is confined to the margins of streams, and the low grounds, where it is partially or wholly concealed, until the overlooking eminence is reached. Again, God has provided three important and complete substitutes for timber and wood. At almost every point in the bluffs, just where it is most convenient and yet out of the way, is an abundance of limestone and sandstone, of a most excellent quality for buildings or for fences. Coal has been found at several points already, lying bare where it crops out in the bluffs, and indications of its presence are abundant throughout the Territory; and the Osage orange grows in perfection, from which an impervious hedge is formed the third year.

In such a country, thus supplied, neither a log-cabin nor a rail fence should ever be built. For fences, the Osage orange will probably be found, in general, the cheapest, as well as the most beautiful material. Yet in very many locations, stone fence can be constructed, as is believed, at one dollar per rod, and this has one great advantage over all others, it will stop the prairie fire.

The mound and ditch, or sod fence, has been used in some parts of Missouri and Illinois, but is now very generally abandoned for the Osage hedge. It is said that a fence, woven from small hemp-cord, with meshes of about five inches, has been introduced in England, as a substitute for wire fences. It is saturated with some preparation of pitch, which preserves it from the effects of the atmosphere, and is sufficiently strong. From the fact that it can be prepared and immediately put up, it may perhaps be worthy of a trial, at least as a temporary fence, while hedges are growing. The manufacture of this netting is a very simple matter, and it is also said that it will furnish a very cheap fence.

There is evidently no necessity for consuming the timber of the country for fences, nor for being dependent upon the owners of timber, for this purpose. Nothing but a present and unavoidable necessity should induce a settler to erect a log-cabin in such a country as Kansas. In the first place, a comfortable log house, if such a thing can be, is a costly structure, and secondly, the useless waste of timber, as compared with a light and suitable frame, "*balloon-frame*," is enormous. At the Catholic mission, on the north side of the Kansas, we were informed by the lady in whose house we passed the night, that a log room twelve by fifteen, which she put up as an addition, cost her $70. A double log house, that is, with two rooms, a passage, or open space between, the whole forty-five feet long and sixteen feet wide—walls eight feet six inches high, with three doors and three windows, the logs hewn on both sides, with pine floors and doors, cost $594. A common shanty, of the same size, would cost about $150, as we were told.

Such facts, and the importance of being so far as possible independent of the use of timber, should lead the settlers at once to experiments with stone for walls, so abundant and so excellent in its quality, or to the gravel or grout walls, which in some places have been so successfully adopted, and which, from the abundance of material, can be built as cheaply in Kansas as in any spot in the country, or to the wall of sun-dried bricks, or "*adobes,*" made from the prairie soil. We were informed by some who had visited Salt Lake, that the Mormons have built houses from these bricks three stories high, by the use of a stucco or common plaster for the outside, and that such buildings are strong and beautiful.

Most of the cabins in Kansas are pointed up, or "*filled in*" between the logs, with this material. It dries so hard as to ring to the stroke, and we have no doubt that, with bricks from this soil, dwellings much cheaper and much better than log-cabins, can be constructed.

Should the settlers construct their first dwellings either of stone or with gravel walls, or from these adobes, they would be dry and warm, and sickness would in a great measure be avoided.

Sun-dried bricks have been extensively used in the large plains, both of the Old and New world, where timber is scarce, and they will form an available material in Kansas. Still they have not hitherto commended themselves to

American taste or judgment, and perhaps no necessity for their use will ever be found in Kansas.

Should such a policy be adopted in regard to fences and dwellings, there will be found an abundance of timber in the country, and it will continually increase. Timber will spring up everywhere, the moment that the annual prairie fires are checked, and the growth of many kinds of trees is extremely rapid. Cottonwoods have been known, in moist grounds, to grow from twelve to seventeen feet high in a single year, and the black locust shoots up with scarcely less rapidity.

A question, however, still remains. If sawed lumber is used for building, and to some extent for fencing, then at what distance from timber lands can a prairie farm be successfully cultivated? We have inquired of Illinois farmers in regard to this point, and the reply has been that farms, ten or twelve miles from timber, are profitably occupied.

Taking this as a guide, we will turn to Kansas. Our route to Fort Riley lay along the north side of the Kansas, at some distance from the stream, and it crossed the lines of timber on its tributaries. A statement of distances between them will be interesting, as bearing upon this question of timber:

Along the Missouri is a broad line of heavy timber.

From the Mo., westward to Salt creek, is about	4	miles.
Thence to Stranger creek, ...	9	"
Thence to Hickory point, ...	12	"
Thence to Grasshopper, with Slue creek between,	10	"
Thence to Soldier creek, ...	20	"

Thence to the Catholic mission, ... 20 miles.
Thence to Lost creek, ... 7 "
Thence to Vermilion, ... 5 "
Thence to Rock creek, ... 4 "
Thence to Sargent's creek . . . . 13 "
Thence to Big Blue, ... 3 "
Thence to Wild Cat, ... 7 "
Thence to Fort Riley, ... 12 "

Along all this route, to the left, lay also the heavy line of timber on the Kansas, which, though mainly in the possession of the Indians, at present, can be obtained, as is said, at moderate prices.

At fort Riley, as before mentioned, is a very fine body of timber, on the streams that unite to form the Kansas.

From Fort Riley to Council Grove, thirty miles, the route is over the high land which divides the waters of the Kansas from the Neosho and Osage, in the southeast. On this route we crossed Clark's creek, fifteen miles from Fort Riley, which has a narrow line of timber. About ten miles from this we reached the timber on the head waters of the Neosho, in the vicinity of Council Grove. This timber presents a heavy, luxuriant growth, and it becomes more abundant down the streams toward the southeast.

From Council Grove, our route toward Fort Leavenworth was northeast, on the south side of the Kansas; and we crossed creeks and lines of timber as follows:

From Council Gr. to Big John, Spr'g cr'k, is about 2 miles.
Thence to Rock creek, ... 5 "
Thence to Bluff creek, ... 4 "
Thence to One Hundred and Forty-two Mile cr'k, 6 "

Thence to Elm creek, ...	3 miles.
Thence to Onion creek, ...	2 "
Thence to Log Chain creek, ...	2 "
Thence to Soldier creek (estimated), ...	8 "
Thence to Waukereusa (estimated), ...	15 "
Thence to Smith's Ferry, on Kansas, about . .	11 "

Some of the above are small creeks, with only narrow lines of timber, but they are the extreme head springs of the Neosho and Osage. From the point at Smith's ferry where we re-crossed the Kansas, to its mouth, about one hundred miles, the timber is fine, on its bottom lands, and though mostly on the Indian reservations, can, as is said, be cheaply purchased. Of this fact we have no personal, or positive knowledge.

These statements, we think, are sufficient to show that few, if any points in Kansas, are so remote from timber as to be valueless—that, in fact, there need be little apprehension of serious difficulty on this account.

OSAGE ORANGE HEDGE.

To some, perhaps, the following statement, from one who has experience in hedge growing, may be useful:

Plant the seed in a nursery, with the ground *very carefully* prepared. In the following spring (April in Kansas) transplant; cut the young plants close to the ground, or "*down to the yellow bark*," and, on ground prepared with care, and to be kept free from weeds, set them out in diagonal lines, six inches apart, thus . · . · . · . The plants will then shoot out branches thickly, close to the ground, and form an impenetrable fence, sufficient to turn any stock, the third year, and which even in the second year is a good defense. One quart of seed, as is said, properly managed, will produce plants enough for one quarter of a mile of hedge. The seed should be swelled or sprouted before planting.

COST OF A FARM, AND FARMING.

The claim of one hundred and sixty acres, which the settler makes under the pre-emption law, will, when surveyed, cost him, of course, one dollar and twenty-five cents per acre; for this the crops which he will raise, before the land can be entered, will more than pay. The first plowing of the prairie will cost, at present, when men and teams are hired, two dollars and twenty-five cents per acre. All other expenses are incapable of any estimate, as each man will build a dwelling and fences to suit himself; will purchase more or less of farming implements, and of stock, and will surround himself with more or less conveniences, as circumstances allow.

This land, with ordinary cultivation, will produce (according to the care bestowed):

Of corn, from	50 to 100	bushels	per	acre.		
Of oats, say	40 "	"	"	"	"	
Of wheat (average), . . .	20 "	"	"	"	"	
Of potatoes (300 bushels sometimes raised), .	200		"	"	"	
Of hemp, ($120 per ton),	1000 lbs.			"	"	

The prairie affords from one to four tons of hay per acre, according to season and location, which is even now cut, to some extent, with mowing-machines; to the use of which, or of 'reapers,' no obstacle exists. Whatever vegetable or fruit will grow well in New Jersey, Pennsylvania, or Kentucky, may be produced in perfection in Kansas.

In three years after locating upon the open prairie, a man may have his farm surrounded and divided by hedges; his dwelling adorned with shrubbery, and young shade-trees—several kinds of fruit-trees and grape-vines in bearing—and if he pleases, a young forest, already capable of supplying him with some small timber.

For stock, the prairie produces abundance, both of hay and pasturage, and all the cattle which we observed on these prairies were in very fine condition; showing that the prairie grass is more nutritious than we had before supposed. The country seems admirably adapted both to the cultivation of grain and the raising of stock.

The price of horses, oxen, cows, and mules, is about the same as it is in Missouri, Ohio, and Kentucky. The price of corn, wheat, and other grains, is, on account of the drouth, extremely high: corn, one dollar and fifty cents per bushel; wheat flour, six, to six dollars and twenty-five cents per cwt., and other things in proportion; and at these prices there is a home market for more than has been produced.

Such a state of things will not continue, but a home market for the productions of Kansas will be found, for a long period, at prices equal to those of the States—and this will make fortunes for those who will be content to enter at once into the steady and systematic cultivation of the soil, instead of being beguiled by the more dazzling *promise*, of the various speculations so common in a newly-opened country. The influx of settlers will, of itself, open and long maintain an extensive market, while its position, in relation to the western government stations, to the California and Oregon emigration, and the Santa Fê trade, will insure, for the farmers of Kansas, a steady cash market at home for whatever they can produce. To this should be added the fact that the manufacturing resources of the country will create, of themselves, an extended home market, of great importance to the agricultural interest.

MINES AND MANUFACTURES.

As has been already stated, bituminous coal, of an excellent quality, seems to abound. The limestone of the country is the carboniferous limestone, and in the bluffs, in various places, it crops out in veins from fifteen, to twenty inches thick; and the indications are, that the quantity is abundant and widely diffused.

It is the same formation as that on the eastern side of the Missouri. The strata, on both sides, dip slightly toward the bed of the river, and on the east side, in Missouri, the beds of coal are thicker, and of better quality as we recede from the river, until some beds in the interior are twelve feet thick. Such was the information given us on the spot.

We should, of course, expect the same in Kansas. As in other parts of the Mississippi valley, the geological formation indicates the existence of iron, which is so abundant in Missouri. Lead has been found: the Indians have brought in specimens of tin, and zinc; and a bed of excellent gypsum has been found on the Smoky Hill fork, above fort Riley. Clay for bricks, and potter's clay, abound, and large beds of copper are said to exist on Turkey creek.

It may be assumed as a settled fact, that the slave States, while they remain such, will never manufacture for themselves; and their helplessness, in this respect, is almost beyond belief. We were informed by a Missourian, a citizen of a town of four thousand inhabitants, on the Missouri, that if a carriage axle was bent or broken, it could not be repaired in the place; if a shaft were broken it could not be replaced; and we were elsewhere informed, that, throughout the beautiful farming region of the Upper Missouri, so far from manufacturing farming implements, not even a plow could be properly repaired.

Such, so far as our observation extended, is the universal state of things. If, therefore, Kansas should become a free State, and attract to herself an emigration which should introduce eastern mechanical skill and experience, she would at once furnish manufactures of wood, iron, leather, hemp, and a countless variety of articles, for an immense country both above and below her, as well as for the government and for the supply of the emigrants' outfit, and the trade to Santa Fé.

Kansas, if free, will be very likely to present a copy of manufacturing New England; nor will the water-power, the mineral wealth, and the timber, on her western district, at the base of the Rocky mountains, always lie beyond the reach of her population.

CHAPTER XII.

A NIGHT ON THE BANKS OF THE BIG BLUE.

THROUGH one beautiful afternoon we had traveled over the billowy prairie that seemed to be steeped in sunbeams, and toward evening, as the sun was sinking into the flood, which himself had poured abroad, presenting a scene equal in glory to any sunset at sea; a dark-blue line, stretching along the expanse, and looking like the coast in the far distance over water, showed us that we were approaching the "timber" that skirts the banks of the Big Blue, the largest and most beautiful tributary of the Kansas.

As we descended from the high prairie into these timber bottoms, we found a thick growth of tall and thrifty trees, oaks, elms, cottonwoods, sycamores, mingled with hickory and ash, forming a wide grove on either side of the stream.

Our road, for a time, lay along the foot of a high, and almost overshadowing bluff, while below us, through the dark arches of the trees, we could see the broad river, rippling in its flow, and sparkling in the sun, or lying still and dark under the shadow of its western shore, while still beyond, appeared the open and apparently cultivated meadows of the prairie, extending far as the eye could reach.

The evening song of birds broke sweetly the general

silence; here and there a squirrel dropped down the nuts he was gathering, and quails and prairie hens would cast on us an inquiring glance, and then away to cover. It seemed almost impossible to believe that we were not in some old and highly-cultivated country; we could scarce help expecting that we should soon be among orchards, and grain-fields, and elegant dwellings.

We reached, at dusk, a log-cabin of somewhat more than the ordinary pretensions, *three stories long*, and one story high, around which was a paling fence, formed of split sticks, indicating that the march of civilization had begun, and that the first stage, that of the rail or worm fence, for the front yard, had here been already passed. Seldom is a more beautiful site for a dwelling seen. In the rear, the sheltering bluffs threw round it a protecting wall of green, while in front was the bright, clear river and its broad, natural meadows. It will probably be spoiled, for it offers an advantageous location for a "tavern," and rum and tobacco, and drunken swearing men will very soon be there, to mar the beauty of the works of God. We found that the three stories were not too many for the accommodation of the owners. They formed quite a patriarchal family, well suited to the Oriental-looking pastures and meadows that lay around them. Jacob, himself, had scarcely more sons and daughters, and sons-in-law and daughters-in-law, children, and grandchildren, than were gathered here.

Supper was provided, and we sat down in the midst of the family, there being no alternative, unless we, or the family, should occupy the outside of the house, during the meal. The patriarch, himself, who had been absent, returned just at this juncture, and seated himself with us. I inquired if he had any objection to my asking God to bless our food. He readily assented, but a marked change at once came over him.

His wife, who was sitting near me, said that they had lost all "their manners" since they came out to Kansas. The "old man," she added, "used to say grace, before he came out here, but since we came to this place he has lost his manners." The old man seemed to lose "his manners" in another sense, after this frank confession of his wife. He was moody during the meal, and answered us rather gruffly, in some things. We were soon shown the room where we were to sleep. Some of the party had begun to lay aside their garments, when he walked in with his pipe in his hand, a most capacious one, filled it, lighted it at the candle, and sat down as if he felt at home, in his own house, unmindful of the turning down and tucking up of bed-clothes, and the half undressed condition of his guests. Something evidently was lying with great weight on his mind. He smoked with nervous energy, while it was clear that his conversation was only a skirmishing of outposts, a prelude to something which he had not yet got at. Boots were drawn off, cravats were laid aside, suspenders even unbuttoned, but the patriarch comprehended not. Smoke now filled the room so that one of the party was absolutely "smoked out," and was obliged to seek the open air. I suggested to the old man that the tobacco had sickened him.

It took him quite by surprise. It had not even occurred to him that anybody could dislike tobacco. As to the idea that his presence in our sleeping apartment was an intrusion, I saw that he could never be made to comprehend that, and what sort of a writ of ejectment could be served upon him was becoming a serious question, and though much amused, we were also not a little annoyed.

He finally marched straight up to the matter that was pressing upon his mind. He turned to me and asked, "Are you a preacher?" Considering my external man, resembling a Californian, when "*prospecting*," more than a minister, I honored the old man for his doubts. I think he only partly believed me when I answered, "Yes." "I wish you had got here," he replied, "before sundown, I would have sent round and had 'em come in to hear you preach."

He then said that he was a member of the Methodist church, and used once to enjoy religion, and had family prayers, and grace at the table, but since he had come into Kansas he had become cold and neglectful, and he had, he said, a great many about him who were not Christians, and he found it hard to live in a Christian way. His case was now perfectly clear. He was rebuked and mortified by what had occurred at the table, his spiritual nakedness had been revealed to strangers, and the aroused conscience had compelled him to come to us, and make explanations.

He could not rest until he had partially unburdened his spirit. His Christian graces had not well endured the transplanting into Kansas, and lacking the support of the usual external helps, they had well-nigh perished entirely.

He was one of a very numerous class of professors whose piety depends very much upon circumstances, and who, without the presence of a ministry, and the ordinances of a church, exhibit neither life nor light. The new States and the Territories swarm with such dead or frozen disciples, and the sad fact shows the great importance of the emigration of Christian colonies, of *churches*, by which many weak ones might be kept from falling, and perhaps strengthened in the faith.

The old man in the end expressed a wish to call his family together for evening worship, and gladly resuming the garments which had been laid aside, we followed him back to our dining-room, which was at once filled by the numerous tribe, and a scene somewhat vexatious in its commencement, was interesting and solemn in its close. The next morning he was reminded of the importance of his position, at the head of so large a household, whose views of religion would be greatly influenced by his example. We found that other professors were living in the vicinity, and urged upon him the duty of at least endeavoring to assemble on the Sabbath for prayer-meeting. He replied, "As soon as these soldiers get away I shall try and do something,"

We learned then that some soldiers from a neighboring fort were engaged on a government work near by; that they boarded with him; that his piety had not the courage to show itself in their presence, and Satan had persuaded him to wait until he could be pious without an effort, and without the necessity of bearing his cross.

A man does not escape from himself by a journey to Kansas, and Satan follows the weak and wavering Christian even into the wilderness. Our old friend is, I think, a child of God, but he lacks the manly courage which is one of the brightest excellencies of the Christian character when the energy is tempered with meekness. Thousands, not in

Kansas, are waiting until the *soldiers are gone*, before they attempt their duty.

The night spent at the Big Blue was a cloudless one, and the purity of the atmosphere, in Kansas, was beautifully exhibited by the exceeding brilliancy of the heavens. Never before was my soul so filled, and even awed by the glory of the skies. I had never before felt so deeply the loveliness of perfect purity as in looking at the milky-way that night—so stainless, so perfectly defined, and yet with so soft an outline. It surely needs the knowledge of the one true God. to prevent man, in such a climate, from worshiping the stars. To show the effect of the scene upon a youthful mind I insert here an extract from the journal of the youngest member of the party:

"THE HEAVENS AT BIG BLUE.

"All day we had traveled amid scenes of wonderful beauty. We journeyed toward the setting sun, and often ere he sank into the plain, he drew our eyes to where the lengthening shadows, stretching away from every rock, and knoll, and tree, were pointing back to our eastern homes. Strangers, and in a strange land, memory had little need of being thus aroused, for although our faces were set westward, our hearts went quickly home, and our spirits heard the voices of those we loved, and we saw their familiar faces.

"Slowly the sun withdrew through gates of gold, that were surrounded by a deeper, purer blue, than I had ever seen before. The glowing sky was so clear, so stainless, that it seemed as if the gates of Paradise were partly opened, and the *shadow* of that heavenly radiance whose splendor mortality can not bear, was lighting up the scene. The mind, unless altogether earthly, is always deeply impressed by the closing up of a summer-day. The sinking sun, the deepening twilight, the gradual coming of the stars in their appointed order, and the stretching of the milky-way across the sky, will always affect one, even amid the dust and smoke of a city, but situated as we were, beyond the very borders of civilization, and almost beyond the abodes of men, the death of that calm, beautiful day, came like a sweet spell over the heart. Night came, clothed, as it seemed, in her "festal garments;" she had put on all her stars. Above, the heavens glowed, and below, every blade of grass, and every little leaflet, sparkled also with its star-drop of dew.

"The outline of the distant prairie, as it rose and fell, *apparently* against the sky, rounding into all conceivable curves of beauty, was in itself a magnificent picture, and yet but a single feature in the scene which God had there unrolled. I did not wonder, as my eye wandered over the magnificence of *these* heavens, that the heathen, in more southern climes, should nightly bow himself to worship in such a temple, whose walls rise higher than the "armed eye" can reach, and whose pavements are stars, and firmaments of stars. It is not strange that these glorious lights before the throne should be mistaken for the Divinity himself.

"Among the mountains of New England, I had looked on the same scene, and again, I had watched these stars while floating on the bosom of the upper lakes, and often from the hills around our Queen City, I had endeavored, by the aid of man's short-sighted wisdom, to search out these hidden mysteries of God.

"At these three, widely separated points, the heavens had presented the same scene to my eye, but now it was essentially changed. As an old painting is improved by cleansing and restoring what has faded, so it seemed to me, that, compared with what I had seen before, some hand had freshly burnished the whole vault of heaven, and brightened all its jewels. The blue of the sky was dark, almost to blackness, and the stars seemed nearer, larger, and more lustrous. With the sleeping prairie, silent and uninhabited, around, and so pure a sky above, I thought I could imagine the beauty of earth ere man had marred its loveliness, and I turned forward to that new creation, when it shall be swept and garnished again. With what feelings I beheld, so far from home, each familiar shining one. Far in the East I had hailed their appearance, nightly, and watched and followed them with my glass, and now, as old acquaintances, they were doubly welcome, where all was strange and earthly friends were few. Arcturus looked down with eye as fiery, as when the Patriarch mentioned him in his hymn, worshiping 'Him who guideth Arcturus and his sons;' the Northern Crown was slowly setting, bending to place its coronet upon the prairie's brow, and Cassiopeia rode on in queenly magnificence. On how many crumbling thrones had she looked down, since God first sent her forth along her shining way! 'Time writes no wrinkle on her changeless brow.' There, too, were the folding coils of The Serpent, sparkling with many hues, as if trying the arts of fascination. Aquarius was there, but it was only in mockery that he seemed to lavish the contents of his ample vase, upon the parched earth. The Heavenly River, (Eridanus) rolling its waters westward, reminded me of the 'streams' that 'shall make glad the city of our God.'

"The Eagle and The Youth were pursuing their journey, side by side, symbolizing, as I thought, the great future of this West. To an American the eagle speaks of republicanism and civilization in its highest form—of a great and prosperous nation. The western youth has joined hands with the eagle, and together they are starting on their way. May the splendor of the heavenly pair be typical of the result on earth. Again, the silvery beauty of Altair brought up a crowd of familiar faces, with whom, at home, I had often looked upon his brightness. Blue eyed Lyra 'discoursed sweet music' from her golden harp. The wolves on the prairies seemed to be howling praises to their fellow Wolves, that had been, by the ancients, enthroned among the stars. I thanked God for these smiles of my starry friends, and laid up, among the treasures of memory, that night scene on the banks of the Big Blue."

CHAPTER XIII.

THE SCENERY OF THE PRAIRIES—THE PAST, THE PRESENT, THE FUTURE.

I HAVE before stated that the Kansas prairies are indescribable, and this is true. Yet when the spirit has been deeply moved by any object, we can scarce refrain from an attempt, however feeble and unsuccessful, to describe the scene to others, that they may share in our emotions. This induces me to speak again of the scenery of the prairies. I have just reached an elevated spot, the top of one of the prairie billows that has heaved itself above its fellows. From this low eminence let us look around. The eye sweeps, without one obstruction, round a perfect circle of at least fifty miles in diameter. Everywhere the undulating outline of the plain touches the "horizon's rim." Over the vast plateau the heavens seem spread out on purpose to curtain it in; a dome "whose maker and builder is God," and which, glowing, as it is, with excess of light, seems to send down to us the glory of some "upper sky," the *shining through* of a heavenly splendor.

Much has been said of the awe one feels beneath the center of the dome of St. Peter's, but here we are under a dome whose base is fifty miles across, and which swells, measureless, into the height of the heavens. Below it, seems a vast amphitheater; for from the horizon's edge the prairie appears to slope gently inward toward the center, so that the boundary line of vision seems to lie on the crest of surrounding hills. But this is a delusion. It is only the general outline of the plain that lies clearly defined against the distant sky. The river bluffs, themselves, seldom rise above the general level of the high rolling plateau. Far, to the south and southwest of us, the line of timber that marks the position and course of the Kansas, appears like a long blue cloud, just resting on the boundless meadows. West of us, a slender, silver line runs across the prairie, for many a mile, and loses itself in the distance. 'Tis the mist which, after a shower whose clouds are gone, is rising over the channel of one of the tributaries of the Kansas, coming in from the north. It looks almost as if the milky-way had descended to the earth, and was now floating slowly back to the skies.

The distant river sweeps close up to the base of the bluffs, and they present many grand and curious features as they swell out into the river valley, and where their upper outline stands out against the sky. They appear in the distance much more abrupt than they are in reality. To the eye they rise from the edge of the valley, almost as steeply as walls—but walls of most huge dimensions. They look like immense fortifications. It would not surprize us to behold there the floating folds of banners, nor to see gigantic sentinels pacing their rounds on those battlements. That long regular slope, rising from the river, looks indeed, like a *glacis*, constructed with military precision;

those huge, rounded promontories, reaching out into the valley, might well be taken for bastions, and that level line, that for so many miles stretches along the sky, looks like the graded top of the parapet.

Yonder, too, are circular mounds, cone-shaped and isolated, regular in form as if art had constructed them, yet not artificial, commanding a view of the whole adjacent country to the limits of vision, while on the top of one appears a smaller cone, as if it were crested with a watch-tower. From these various elevations and projections, huge shadows, as the sun declines, are thrown over the long slopes and level prairie, adding still to the variety and beauty of the scene.

Now let the eye range round the circumference of this circle—one hundred and fifty miles, at the very least. See this plain around us—fifty miles, or more, across. It seems, at first glance, a country full of people, so evident, so universal appear to be the evidences of cultivated life. We think we see countless meadows and grain-fields all about us. We have not closely observed, but surely here must be a multitude of flocks, and "cattle on a thousand hills." We look for the spires of distant villages—the snowy gleam of white dwellings under the low, green hills, we listen for the voices of human life. We start at the result. Not a single human dwelling can the eye detect in all the vast amphitheater; not even a smoke curls up anywhere to tell of life; not a sound can be heard, beyond ourselves, that indicates the presence of man. Not even an Indian is abroad, in all the prairie. There may, or may not be, a log-cabin or two, somewhere within this circle, but, so far as eye or ear can determine, it is one immense waste, and voiceless solitude, hushed into the very silence of the tomb. Here, away as we are from the groves by the river, there 's not a leaf to rustle, nor a bird to sing. Yonder hawk waves his wings all silently as he floats along, and the ear, pained with the intense stillness, is relieved by even the buzzing of a fly. "Where are the people?" Few have ever looked upon these prairies, I think, without being constrained to ask this question. We seem not disposed to doubt that the whole scene was once throbbing with the pulse of a great people's life. We feel that in some way they have suddenly vanished, and we ask, Will they re-appear, or are the multitudes of their dead sleeping around us; has this great silence fitly settled here, over a nation's tomb? In this case, where God has not yet seen fit to disclose one of the most interesting secrets of the past, each one may indulge his own conjecture, if not plainly contrary to the teaching of existing facts.

For myself I was constrained to adopt, at once, the opinion of those who believe that the prairies are the once cultivated fields of a race that has passed away, and left no representative behind. The mounds, the remains of fortifications, and apparently of walled cities; the ruined temples of Central America, and these green fields now empty and silent, seem to be joint memorials of a common past—and of that past the prairies are, to me, the most solemn and touching monument. In a region desolated by war, the fragments of demolished temples, and the shattered walls of forts, are not the saddest features in the scene.

The *country*, emptied of its inhabitants, despoiled of its

flocks and herds, its orchards and vineyards ruined, and far and wide, its fields unoccupied, lying waste and silent, this is more deeply affecting. So, in looking at the prairies, we feel that all around us there were once multitudes of happy homes; that millions once dwelt on these broad plains, devoted to the gentle arts of peace, and elevated far above the condition of the wandering savage; that these were their grain-fields and pasture-grounds; that their flocks, and herds, and vineyards were on these hill-sides; that this impressive stillness is the silence of death, and this rank grass is growing over forgotten graves—its very rankness suggesting that the plains may have once been fertilized with blood, and the ashes of the dead. In the period in which those builders of temples, cities, and mounds dwelt here, this continent lay, it seems, without the range of *that* world which alone has furnished materials for history; and here a western world, with empires of its own, populous as those by the Euphrates or the Nile, the Egean or the Tiber, has had its life of centuries, which no poet has sung, or historian recorded. One of those great revolutions has occurred here, such as left the plain of Shinar and the valley of the Nile almost as desolate as the prairie; a great multitude has been swept out of existence, a race has perished, and God has sealed up the secret of its history, so that no man can open.

It seems scarcely possible to entertain the idea, that the present race of Indians are the descendants of those who built the mounds and temples. Every known characteristic forbids the supposition. There 's not a single feature in all their mental structure, there 's nothing in their tastes or modes of life whatever, that would suggest such a previous existence as some race must have had in this central garden-land of America.

Their whole appearance is that of the degenerate children of a wild, conquering race; that having overrun a cultivated country, and swept the inhabitants away, and incapable of any organization or progress, separated into roving bands, and warring upon each other, nourished the heart of slaughter and revenge, and sunk at last to where the white man found them. It seems contrary to the whole course of human development, that such a race as the Indians of our country could have descended from those who worshiped in these ornamented temples whose ruins remain—dwelt in these cities whose walls are not wholly gone, and cultivated these plains.

They present two distinct and antagonistic phases of national life—the one must have destroyed and succeeded the other. The present Indian is the Scythian of the west.

This race also has nearly finished its course. As surely as races, like individuals, have characteristics peculiar to themselves, capacities which indicate fitness or unfitness for certain modes of thought or action, so certain does it appear that the Indian race will never assume the forms of the Anglo-Saxon civilization; and it is difficult to conceive how any one who has visited the tribes in their homes, can reach a different conclusion. The fond anticipations which many are indulging of Christianized and civilized Indian nations, on our western borders, will, in all probability, never be realized. The preaching of the Gospel will doubtless secure the salvation of individuals; many may thus be gathered as trophies of the abounding grace of God, but the civilization of the nineteenth century is not for them. As a people, the Gospel will not save them. As a race, and nationally, they are lost already, and will disappear. They have played their part through, in the world's development, and they are nearly ready to leave the stage. As they succeeded to the position of a vanishing race, so we have done to theirs. Their stewardship is over and their doom pronounced, and ours is now beginning. The dominions of the Toltecans have, through the red tribes, come down to us, and the prairies of Kansas, and those adjoining, will soon present all the forms of a new life—the life of the nineteenth century—and that peculiar form of it which God has committed to the American people; for even Anglo-Saxon civilization has an American phase. Should we permit slavery to enter here with abominations more hideous in the sight of God than those of the savages, will he not even take the kingdom from us?

CHAPTER XIV.

TOWN SITES AND SETTLEMENTS.

In the few days only that have elapsed since the following chapter was written, some progress has been made in the settlement of the Territory, and in determining the sites of future towns. Still, I have thought best to let it remain as originally penned, for it will at least show how far the first impressions of the Commissioners sent, are confirmed by subsequent events. The New England settlement on the Waukereusa, has since received some large accessions, and the first number of a paper, a large, fine-looking sheet, and devoted to the cause of freedom, has been issued there. A large colony, as is said, has selected Council Grove as its center, and some claims have been made in the vicinity of Fort Riley.

The natural features of the country would seem to point out the necessity of three, perhaps four, principal commercial centers for Kansas, as points for exchange between herself and other States, viz: one in the neighborhood of St. Joseph; one near the mouth of the Kansas river; one on her southeastern border, where it will be touched by the Southwestern Branch Railway from St. Louis toward Texas; and *perhaps* a fourth somewhere in the valley of the Arkansas.

All speculations, except of quite a general character, concerning town sites in a country so little known as Kansas, must necessarily be somewhat vague, yet perhaps the public are entitled to the opinions of the Commissioners, though the immediate future may show them to be erroneous. A central city at, or near the mouth of the Kansas, *may*, by means of railways running west, northwest and southwest, concentrate on that single point, nearly the whole commerce of the Territory.

Be this as it may, enterprise, competition, and the spirit of speculation are already busy with cities and city lots. A city called Atchison has already been laid off, not far below St. Joseph, on the Missouri, with an eye to the trade of the upper division of Kansas, on the Nemaha, Wolf creek, and the upper waters of the Big Blue and Vermilion rivers.

Three miles below Fort Leavenworth, and some twenty-five miles above the mouth of the Kansas, is Leavenworth City. The proximity of Fort Leavenworth, and the supposed presence of the Territorial Government near, may be circumstances in its favor, but it is not located at the point toward which the commerce of the Territory would naturally flow. That point is at the mouth of the Kansas, and to it trade will flow as naturally as the waters of the river.

There is already, Kansas City, but it is in Missouri, whose boundary here touches the western shore of the Missouri river. There is a site for a city on the north side of the Kansas, at its mouth, on lands now owned by the Wyandots. It would seem that the commercial capital of Kansas must be at the mouth of its principal stream.

In the southeastern district, through which the Neosho and

the Osage rivers flow, there are as yet few settlers, and no movement has been made toward the building of a city. The prevailing opinion with them seemed to be, that their trade must connect itself with the Kansas valley. If so, it must, of course, be by the common roads, or railways.

In regard to internal towns, the settlers, thus far, have been guided by the very natural idea, that a town would spring up, either at, or near, where the principal streams and valleys strike the Kansas, or are crossed by the main lines of road—such as the Oregon, California, and Santa Fé routes. At all such points, especially along the north shore of the Kansas, settlements have been formed, and claims have been made, for some distance up the streams, and to the depth of two or three claims, along the main road, in the vicinity of the supposed town site, while back from the streams, and between town locations, the prairie is as yet mostly unclaimed. Thus, commencing on the Missouri and following the Fort Riley road, on the north side of the Kansas, we find, first, Leavenworth City; then, westward, are settlements at Salt creek, Hickory Point, Stranger creek, Grasshopper river, Soldier creek, Catholic Mission, Lost creek, Vermilion, Rock creek, Big Blue (the largest tributary of the Kansas, and about one hundred and fifty feet wide, clear and rapid), Wild Cat creek, and Fort Riley.

Then from Council Grove toward the Missouri, and the mouth of the Kansas, settlements have been made in the same manner, on the creeks heretofore mentioned as the tributaries of the Neosho and Osage, where these are crossed by the Santa Fé road. The same process is also going forward in the northern district, on Wolf creek, the

Nemaha, and on the upper waters of the Vermilion and Big Blue rivers; a settlement of some importance having already been made by a company, where the government road to forts Kearney and Laramie crosses the Big Blue.

Among all these, will there be any important towns? A question which time, alone, can answer satisfactorily; yet some suggestions may not be entirely useless. One fact should, we think, be considered. The Indian reservations lie along the Kansas, running back from six miles to ten miles, and many spots, now chosen for towns, lie outside of the boundaries of these Indian lands, and consequently six and ten, or more miles, from the mouths of the streams on which they are located. These Indian reservations will not always be Indian lands, and when they, also, are open for settlement, will not the true business centers be found further down, where these valleys and streams meet the Kansas, whether this stream proves to be navigable, or whether a railway is constructed along its banks?

Doubtless, on all of these streams, small towns will spring up, but there seemed to us some special attractions on the Grasshopper, a clear and beautiful stream, about eighty-five feet wide, and a site for a still larger town on the Big Blue, a clear, swift stream, one hundred and fifty feet wide, even in the drouth. On the lower part of this river few claims had been made at the time of our visit, (September).

The confluence of the two important streams that form the Kansas, and the beauty and fertility of their valleys, as well as the large body of timber at Fort Riley, indicate that spot as the site of an important place, while a town will also be established at, or near, Council Grove. This is in the midst of a fertile and beautiful region.

Without railways, or the navigation of the Kansas, towns at the mouth of the Big Blue, at Fort Riley, and Council Grove, would be situated very much as Columbus, in Ohio, Harrisburgh, in Pennsylvania, Utica, in New York, and Springfield, in Massachusetts, once were; though the natural roads in Kansas are superior to any artificial ones we ever saw, and the small quantity of rain which falls in the winter months is not sufficient to render them muddy. They are so, only for a short time, in the spring. Should these towns, however, become the radiating points for railways, like so many interior towns of the north and east, their future can be easily foreseen.

Will there be an interior town of importance on the Kansas, between its mouth and Fort Riley? These points are about one hundred and forty miles apart. About midway between them, on the south side of the Kansas, and on the peninsula between it and the Waukereusa, the New England settlement has been established, and twenty miles beyond, up the river, is Stinson's settlement, where a town has lately been laid out, which is called Tecumseh. The trade of the region of Council Grove could reach a point on the Kansas, about half way from its mouth to Fort Riley, either by the common road, or by a railway, with about half the distance now traveled, viz: from Council Grove to the Missouri.

This would probably be true, also, of a portion of the trade of the Big Blue and Vermilion. If, then, a town at such a point on the Kansas, could avail itself, either of the navigation of the river, or connect itself with the Missouri by railway, it would, of course, become one of the most important interior towns of Kansas.

At such a point the New England settlement has been established, and we presume that those interested will not fail to avail themselves of all the advantages of their position. This Company will soon demonstrate the advantages of combination of capital and skill in the settlement of a new country. They have selected one of the most beautiful locations in the Territory, lovely enough to satisfy the most fastidious taste, and commanding a wide view of the surrounding country. From observations made on the spot, we think the plan has been wisely conceived, and though the work has been delayed, somewhat, beyond early anticipations, is now being pushed on with system and energy. A plot, equal to about two miles square, has been reserved for the town; a township organization has been effected; the two first companies have united their interests, and on the day we visited the settlement, there was an auction sale of the *choice* of *claims*. Fifty-six choices were sold, which brought a premium of five thousand dollars. This fact is a sufficient answer to the idle stories which have been put in circulation about the dissatisfaction and return of the New England emigrants. There are now at this point, as is supposed, about four hundred persons.

Two steam saw-mills are ready for business, and machinery for various other purposes will be run by these engines. The Company will be able to supply the emigrants with lumber, at about ten dollars per thousand, and it is hoped that the tents will be exchanged, not for log-cabins, but for comfortable framed dwellings, before the setting-in of winter. A printing-press, driven by steam, is said to be at work; a building for schools, with an upper hall for public worship, is to be erected at once, and the Company will supply the settlers there, with food, and all necessaries, at much lower rates than they could procure them for themselves—a point of great importance during the present scarcity and high prices. In addition, this company has purchased a large hotel in Kansas City, where emigrants will be received, and we are convinced that they are carrying out, in good faith, to the great benefit of the settlers, and with ultimate advantage to the stockholders, the designs which they originally formed.

In the course of a few months, there will be found there, a modern town, with its church, or churches, schools, newspapers, stores, mechanics' shops, and manufacturing establishments, surrounded by a farming population. For the present, we are told, a town lot will be donated to any one who will occupy and improve.

The *present* promise of this spot, is far greater than that of any other in Kansas. Here, the settler will find, almost at once, the privileges and advantages of an older community, and here capital and combination will create business, and attract a population with a continually increasing power—while the advance in price of such land as the Company reserves, will remunerate, as it should do, the holders of its stock.

The noble work, which this Company has undertaken, may be done in a similar manner at many other points, especially at Council Grove and Fort Riley, and by other associations; and we hope to see this general plan acted upon until Kansas is occupied and filled. It strips emigration of its terrors, and renders the settling of a new country a safe, easy, and profitable operation, even for the pioneers.

CHAPTER XV.

THE FIRST WINTER MAY BE ONE OF HARDSHIP.

It will probably prove a fortunate circumstance that no greater number have been able to enter Kansas during the present season. The prices of provisions, necessarily high in the interior, have been largely increased in consequence of the drouth; and the settlers will meet the double difficulty of high prices and scarcity of food.

At the New England settlement these difficulties will be in good degree obviated by the capital and providence of the company, but unless the settler has more than usual resources at command, he may find serious inconveniences during the coming winter. Add to this that the navigation of the Missouri is often interrupted by ice early in November, and we certainly have reason to fear that those who after this period, leave this fall, for Kansas, may meet with unexpected discouragements.

Nor is it the work of a few days only, to make comfortable provision for a dwelling, and other necessary things, and sickness will be the almost inevitable consequence of exposure in tents, and half-finished cabins, of green logs. Already remittent fevers had made their appearance among the settlers, at some points, when we were there, owing entirely to exposure in unsuitable habitations.

There is every reason to suppose that Kansas is eminently healthy, but the settler must not expect that he and his family can escape disease in circumstances which would prove fatal to an ox.

It would not be surprising, therefore, if, during the coming winter, and the next spring, we should hear an evil report concerning the land. Some Missourians were, in September, uttering prophecies, born of their desires, that the "'northwesters' would blow the Yankees away." This will doubtless be true of some. Many have gone into Kansas with no preparation or fitness for the life of pioneers, impelled by the mere spirit of adventure, and with no definite purpose of any kind. They have floated into Kansas on the tide, and on the first slight ebb will float out again, or retire in disgust, if not allowed, in some manner, to prey on the community. Let no one be deterred by evil reports or croaking prognostications. The land is a good land, eminently so; and considering its advantages, as a whole, they are greater than were ever before offered to the American settler.

Nor should individuals fear that if they delay until next spring, the land will all be occupied, and that good locations can not then be obtained. It is not unlikely that it will be more easy to obtain farms in the vicinity of present settlements, than it is even now. The experience of a winter, in such circumstances as have been described, will discourage many—and their claims will be for sale at a premium less than the sum it would cost to spend the winter in the Territory. There are, moreover, thousands of fictitious claims, which, of course, will never be entered in a land-office. These must be exposed, in a few months, and can be obtained. It was the opinion of experienced men that the early part of the coming spring will be the most favorable time which will ever present for entering the eastern division of Kansas. Nor because colonies are already located in important positions, should it be supposed, that no other suitable positions remain unoccupied.

A colony, such as ought to be formed, wherever the thing is attempted, can, as yet, create an important town at any point in Kansas, where it may choose to locate. Such are the natural features of the country, that around any center which a prudent man would select, in that enormous plain, there would be found the elements for the support of a town, both agricultural and manufacturing. The superiority of one point over another, will depend more upon the capital, skill and enterprise, which may gather there, and upon the character of the population, than upon mere locality. This will prove especially true in regard to the town sites of the interior. Of all these, the position of Fort Riley is most clearly marked by its natural advantages. The confluence of those rivers, forming the Kansas, indicates a town—especially if it should prove the head of navigation on the Kansas. In the wide region around Council Grove, the people and their capital will make the town, in any spot for miles in either direction. The same general remarks may be made in regard to large portions of Kansas. Natural features of country will have less influence upon town sites and their destiny, than in regions where these features are more strongly marked. The truth and importance of this remark will be more clearly seen, if we consider that the abundance of coal and iron, to say nothing of other minerals, affords the means of creating a manufacturing town on almost any spot where a company may pitch their tents.

A small part only has yet been explored, its resources are, as yet, mostly unknown, and the field, either for individual enterprise or for the establishment of colonies, is yet as wide and as inviting as the heart of man ought to desire.

CHAPTER XVI.

FORT RILEY—INDIAN FIGHTING.

About the middle of a very beautiful day, we came in sight of Fort Riley. Standing on a broad, low eminence, swelling gently up from the Kansas valley, on the east, and from that of the Republican on the south, and southwest, its cluster of white buildings presented a neat and attractive appearance; and doubtless the beauty of the picture was enhanced, in our eyes, because we had lately looked only on unsightly cabins. It was a sweet-looking "*oasis*," not indeed a green spot merely, amid sands, but a little "isle of beauty," rising out of the prairie ocean, bright with a *civilized smile*, and wearing the decorations of taste and skill.

It is a new station, established only last November (1853), and hence the freshness of its look; though such is the exceeding purity of the air that many colors will remain long undimmed, even when exposed to the atmosphere, and white walls will not be soon discolored.

Most of the principal buildings have been erected during the present season (1854), and an architect of Cincinnati, as we were told, has left there a lasting evidence of his taste. They are constructed of a limestone which is found in the neighboring bluffs, is easily hewn, and when wrought appears white—a material cheaply obtained, cheaply hewn, and forming a very neat as well as substantial structure. It presents almost the appearance of a chalk formation, inclosing nodules of flint. The same material abounds throughout other portions of the Territory.

On the east lies the Kansas valley, here, perhaps, three miles wide, with its dark-green line of timber, through the openings of which gleams the river, while the eastern bluffs rise quite abruptly, and lie along the sky in bold yet graceful outlines. Toward the Kansas, the eminence on which stand the buildings of the fort, sinks with a very gentle slope. On the west, the land rises to the crest of the bluffs, so as to form, on that side, a sheltering wall. On the south, is the heavy body of timber lying in the forks of the Smoky Hill and Republican—a grove of oaks, elms, sycamores, cottonwoods, and other large timber, here probably three miles wide. The Republican, a broad and rapid stream, comes in from the west, and the Smoky Hill, about two hundred and twenty-five feet wide, flows from the southwest. The water of this stream is quite brackish. Both valleys are beautiful, that of the Republican eminently so near the junction, while we were told by those at Fort Riley, that portions of the valley of the Smoky Hill, are more attractive still. Not a claim had been made, in either valley, at the time of our visit, as was said. From the western bluffs, which we ascended, we could look along the Republican valley, as far as vision could reach, and I could not but feel, as I thought of all the excitement and anxiety, the feverish rush, of city life, that it would be sweet to have a home, a resting-place, in that exquisite solitude, until the speed of life's race could be *slacked*, and the hot machinery of the brain have time to cool. The prairie breeze came and fanned the throbbing brow, as if to show how soothingly the thing could be done, and a hundred times, since my return, when the head has been overwrought, and the heart, too, weary, by night and by day, that beautiful valley has presented itself to the mind, as if it would say, "Come hither and rest!"

A single tent was pitched at the base of the bluff, on the northern side, the evening shadow had begun to soften the outlines of the scene, and a light curling line of smoke, rising from the tent, looked the very symbol of quiet and repose. The tent was occupied by some haymakers from the fort, and one of the number, who has since visited Cincinnati, an intelligent man, informed me that he was so charmed with the spot, that he had selected there his future home.

We were entire strangers at Fort Riley, not having provided ourselves even, with introductions to the officers; but we were received with the open hospitality of the soldier. We were directed to the "quarters" of Lieutenant S., the Quartermaster, to whom we made known our wants, who said, he would at once supply us with suitable "*rations*," a phrase which, at first, almost provoked a smile. We soon found that Uncle Sam feels himself able to "*live well*" in all departments of his great household, and that his "*rations*" are a true *specific* remedy for an appetite. We had the pleasure of meeting at table several of the younger officers of the station, some of them graduates from West Point, and all mingled the bearing of the soldier with the courtesy of the gentleman—ready to show us a kindness, even though it required the temporary surrender of their own comforts.

From these officers, acquainted as some of them were with Indian warfare, we learned many interesting facts, which served to explain the havoc which has sometimes been made with small parties of our troops, in their encounters with the prairie Indians.

We were surprised, incredulous, almost offended, when a young officer, whose eye and bearing certainly showed no lack of courage, deliberately asserted, that our mounted men, though armed with revolvers, were in general not a match, in close combat, for the mounted Indians, with their bows and arrows. But his explanations were satisfactory, and I shall henceforth regard these wild warriors as a formidable foe, even for those who are armed with the most effective weapons of modern times. In the first place, he said, few of the dragoons sent on this service, are trained horsemen; and secondly, the horses, also, are "raw recruits," or at least unused to Indian warfare. On the contrary, the warriors of the prairie are among the most expert riders in the world, and their horses are so thoroughly trained, that they seem to obey even a volition of the rider. They ride without a bridle, guiding the horse by signs, and pressure of the limbs upon his body, leaving both hands free for the use of weapons.

Provided with such a horse, with bow and arrows, and a spear, the Indian, if he finds the opportunity of closing with a dragoon, brings him within range of his arrows, which are effective at a distance of about thirty paces, and rides swiftly around him in a circle, frightening his horse by his yells, so as to render any certain aim with the revolver impossible, while his own arrows are discharged at horse and man more rapidly than even a revolver can be fired. While running round the dragoon in a circle, the Indian will lie along the *outside* of his horse, *lengthwise,* the left leg thrown over the back of the horse, the left arm over the neck, the left hand holding the bow, and with nothing exposed but one leg and one arm, arrows are shot like hail, *from under the horse's neck,* while the animal gallops steadily round and round the victim, who, unable to manage his horse, that is frightened with yells, and maddened with wounds, is too often ingloriously slain by his active and almost invisible enemy.

These Indians of the plain may be called the American Cossack, and are exceedingly troublesome adversaries. Artillery is almost useless in any combat with them, except on rare occasions, as they do not attack in dense bodies, and are able to keep themselves beyond the range of the guns, if they choose.

Perfectly acquainted with the country as they are, they lead our troops into ambuscades, or marching *just ahead* of pursuit, decoy them where no water, or perhaps grass, can be found, except by themselves alone. Seldom attacking, or permitting themselves to be attacked, unless the advantage is greatly on their side, they have cost our country many valuable lives, both of soldiers and among parties of emigrants, and we have reason to fear that the plains toward the Rocky mountains, will yet be the scenes of many fierce encounters.

The melancholy affair at Fort Laramie, where about thirty

soldiers, well armed and with a howitzer, were slain, almost in a moment, by the Sioux, shows what they are capable of doing; though in this case, those who ought to know, declare that the fault was with our soldiers, who began an attack without a cause, and against the dictates of common prudence.

The late massacre, in Oregon, of an emigrant party from Missouri, by the Snake Indians, was made horrible by the very worst atrocities of savage war, for which bloody vengeance will, probably, be taken yet, and we may, perhaps, see another *frontier line* drawn long and broad with blood. It is to be feared, perhaps believed, that most of these Indian murders have been committed on the innocent, in retaliation for injuries received from the whites. The judgment day will bring to light many a bloody deed, perpetrated upon the Indians, in those wide plains, since the over-land emigration to the Pacific began. As an illustration, I will here relate an occurrence, which took place on the banks of the Platte, as described by an eye-witness.

He was one of a company of nearly five hundred, forming one train for California. They generally traveled in small divisions, a little distance apart, for convenience in camping, and in obtaining wood, grass, and water. One morning, while traveling through the Pawnee country, along the bank of the Platte, it was found that the head of the column of wagons had stopped, and, as those in the rear came on, they formed soon a long and solid line. Soon a horseman was sent back from the front, to inform all, that the Pawnees had stopped the train, and demanded tribute, in the shape of cattle, for passing through their country.

The train was stopped, and all flocked, with their rifles, to the front, until several hundred armed men were there. A company of Pawnees had drawn themselves across the road with a chief at their head. They were ordered away—and soon all began to leave but the chief. He drew himself proudly up, and endeavored to bring back and cheer on his warriors. In a moment more he was pierced by fifteen rifle balls. The whole band fled toward the river, but fatally pursued by a volley of balls, a line of dead stretched to the river, and then the whites rushed to the bank, and shot those who were struggling in the water.

It is to be feared that this transaction does not stand alone, and that the prairies have drunk up much Indian blood which is crying in the ear of God—blood wantonly shed without any necessity or even serious provocation. These wandering tribes of the prairie are often sorely pressed by hunger. Driven from their old hunting-grounds, and hemmed in, perhaps, by hostile tribes, they are driven by extremity, and sometimes by the neglect of the Government, to pilfer from the whites, which thefts are not unfrequently atoned for by their blood. It is not unlikely that these Pawnees who demanded the cattle, were destitute of food, and hoped, in this manner, to save themselves from famine, and now, after a wholesale massacre, if one of this tribe should strike down a white, in revenge for some kinsman, shot on the banks of the Platte, the papers will echo round the land, the tale of another Indian murder, and comment upon the diabolical traits of their character.

Their revenge is of the most shocking character, it is true; they seem to be filled with the rage and malignity of devils, but how much worse even this may be in the sight of God, than the cool treachery, the heartless robbery, and needless bloodshed, on the part of the white man, is yet to be determined. With all their hideous features, there are some redeeming traits of nobleness, and there is no sadder sight under the heavens, at present, than they, sunk, as it would appear, where even the mercy of God can not reach them; as *a people* they are oppressed with treachery and power, and driven onward toward annihilation, strike back many a revengeful blow upon those who urge them on. But the abyss yawns across their path, and their final disappearance is near.

We were informed by the officers, of an intention to establish a town on, or near the site of Fort Riley, and that it is the design of the Government, so soon as the settlements in the Kansas valley shall reach upward to the fort, to give up the position, sell out the grounds and buildings, and establish a more western station. Sound policy will doubtless require such a step, and a flourishing city may soon appear at the head of steamboat navigation on the Kansas.

We shall ever remember the kindness and hospitality shown us by the officers at Fort Riley, but to view a soldier's life, and the trade of war through such a medium, would be very much like looking at a slave's life and the system of slavery, from the well-furnished rooms and hospitable board of an intelligent planter, doing all in his power to render your stay agreeable.

While there, we saw, even at this small station, where discipline perhaps, in its strictest forms, is not observed, or needed, enough to convince us that the life of a common soldier borders upon both that of the criminal and slave. Even there, we saw a company driven home from work under the bayonet with cannon balls chained to their legs, and one during our stay endeavored to commit suicide while under confinement for punishment. Another, who had come from the State of New York, gave me to understand that he preferred any position in life where he could be a *freeman*, to the life of a soldier. Said another soldier, just discharged, "Our life is the life of a slave." It will be a joyful day for earth when "the nations shall not learn war any more."

These young officers have since been ordered to Fort Laramie, to engage in that Indian warfare which one of them so graphically described, nor would it be surprising if they, also, should be added to the list of the prairie dead.

CHAPTER XVII.

FROM FORT RILEY TO COUNCIL GROVE—KAW INDIANS.

Fort Riley does not stand, where it is placed on most maps, in the forks of the Republican and Smoky Hill, but on the north bank of the Republican, and perhaps half a mile from the stream. A steam saw-mill has however been erected within the forks, by the Government. The Republican, which is about two hundred feet wide and runs with a rapid current, is spanned by a substantial bridge, while on the road to Council Grove, there is a ferry across the Smoky Hill, whose waters, as I have said, are quite salt to the taste.

After crossing the Smoky Hill, we entered at once the fine grove of timber on its eastern bank, about two miles in width, as we thought, though the road did not cross it at right angles, and we were liable to overrate the distance. It was the merriest and finest woodland scene that we had found in Kansas. The trees were of great size, tall and thrifty, while rank vines and shrubbery of various kinds showed the exuberant fertility of the soil. The trees were filled with a great variety of birds, among which the blue-jay, reminded us most strongly of home, and me, in particular, of that early home of childhood among the hills of New

England, where so often, in the bright mornings of autumn, when the frost had crisped the grass, and clothed the forests in a shroud as gay as if it were a bridal garment, I had listened to that bird, when it was so still that I could hear each falling leaf as it rustled down among the branches, and fell amid its dead companions. And now the cry of that familiar bird, and the blue wings glancing among the leaves, swept space away, rolled back the years, and placed me, where, alas! if I were there, indeed, there would be little to greet me, unless the dead could rise from their graves.

Squirrels seemed to be very happy, while industriously gathering their winter's store; quails would start up, almost from beneath the horses' feet, while a flock of paroquets, chattering above us, reminded me that I was not in New England.

The eastern bluff of the Smoky Hill rises very abruptly, and it was not without difficulty that our two strong horses could drag up it the light wagon which we were using. Once up it, the same seemingly endless, rolling plain, was spread before us, destitute of timber, eastward, to the very limit of vision. This high ground, or "divide," as it is called, between Fort Riley and Council Grove, is, in general, the least attractive of any region which we passed over.

For some fifteen miles it was entirely destitute of timber, and we saw no water by the roadside, though from the undulating character of the prairie, it is not probable that springs were altogether wanting. Parts of this tract are covered with small pebbles, or rather fragments of flint, nodules from the limestone mixed with pieces of the limestone itself, giving the plain, sometimes, where the grass had been lately burned off, a mottled appearance, the white pebbles contrasting with the dark ground. Even here, the soil, though thin, was black, and apparently productive.

About fifteen miles from Fort Riley, is Clark creek. It is a small but very clear and bright little stream, looking like a New England *brook*. It has a narrow bottom, of fine-looking land, where farms might be selected, in a sheltered position, with pastures on the high prairie, above. Crossing Clark creek, we rose again to the higher level, which continued for about eight miles further, when we saw in the far distance, and on a lower level, faint blue lines, which marked the position and course of the head streams of the Neosho and Osage. We soon found ourselves on the crest, if it may be so called, of a broad slope, which sinks downward toward those streams, and a most beautiful region of country was open before us, in which woodland seemed to be sufficiently abundant for life's purposes, and where grain-land and meadows, and hill-side pastures, were ready on all sides for the population to come. Here is one of the finest regions in the Territory for a large colony, and the colony might be large enough to occupy a county. It is about one hundred and thirty miles from Kansas City, and here is the old trading-post, called Council Grove. It is on the great Santa Fé road, and a town in this vicinity would probably become, to a considerable extent, a depot for this southwestern trade, while the agricultural resources of the surrounding country, being almost unlimited, would of themselves support a large inland city. This district of country may have its commercial connection with the Kansas valley, or it may flow southeastward, to the point where the Southwestern Branch Railway will touch Kansas, and thus communicate with St. Louis and the east; while it is possible, that a portion of the commerce of southern and southeastern Kansas may take the direction of Fort Gibson, and the Arkansas valley. There can be no doubt, that a few years will see this fine district thronging with a prosperous population. The mildness of its climate, and the fertility of its soil, will attract a crowd of settlers, so soon as its value is known. The Methodist mission-house, and a few log-cabins, constitute the whole of Council Grove, as it now is, and the site of the present confused "huddle" seems not very happily chosen.

The "Mission" is merely a school, the Kaws not consenting to have the Gospel preached among them. They send a few of their children irregularly to a school, in which little or nothing is, or can be done. The name of "Mission" does not very well describe the thing; and this, we think, is not the only "Mission," in Kansas, to which the same remark would apply. It would do no harm, if this whole subject of Indian missions were somewhat more closely investigated by the Churches. Some unexpected disclosures might be made, perhaps, by such a scrutiny, and the matter would be stripped of much of the heroic, and the romantic, with which it has been so largely invested. Many dreams of Christian Indian nations just budding into life on the frontier, would, probably, be put to flight, by a journey even through Kansas.

We found at Council Grove, about fifteen hundred of the Kaws encamped. A difficulty had arisen between them and the Sauks; one of the Kaws had been killed, and his tribe threatened revenge. It was rumored that the Pottawatomies would join the Sauks, and the Kaws had come in and encamped at Council Grove, with the expectation of greater safety near the Mission, or that they might receive some aid in settling their quarrel. To this we owed the opportunity of seeing, for the first time, a large body of Indians. I had never before seen a community of real, absolute heathen, for such these Kaws are, permitting no Christian teaching among them, except some trifling instruction in reading and writing, to a few of their children. They are among the lowest and poorest of the Indian tribes—guilty of all the vices that Paul ascribes to heathenism, in the first chapter of Romans—and if any new wickedness has been invented since Paul wrote, they doubtless have learned even that. In observing these miserable creatures, I was moved, sometimes to laughter and sometimes with pity, for their ignorance of all good, and consequent wretchedness. In them, sin had wrought out, without much restraint, its legitimate consequences, and they afforded the most fearful evidence of its nature, and its power. No such illustration of the character of man, as he is when left to himself, had fallen under my eye before, and it enabled me to estimate, as I had not previously done, what Christianity has already accomplished for the world, even where most of its influences are merely collateral. The difference between an encampment of these heathen Kaws, and a Christian community, no mathematics can calculate. The scene was enough to stagger one's belief in the unity of the race, and I must confess that my brotherly feelings required a little nursing, a little application of Christian philosophy as a stimulant; and I cannot declare, with truth, that I felt any of the movings and yearnings of that mysterious affection which, it is said, will attract kindred to each other, although personally strangers. I must acknowledge, that my heart did not gravitate very strongly toward my brothers and sisters, of the Kaw branch of the family. I believe, most fully and firmly, in the unity and brotherhood of the race, but I found it difficult to get "*a realizing sense*" of this Kaw relationship.

Man is a sorrowful sight, when he has fallen so low that there is no sublimity in his ruin; and it magnifies, beyond measure, the riches of the grace of God—the *power* as well as the love exhibited in the Gospel—that it can arrest the lowest in his fall, and however degraded and polluted he may be, can re-create, elevate, and refine him, until he becomes fit to associate with angels, and to stand in the presence of God. From such considerations, with a company of heathen before us, we are led to *feel* that the Gospel is a resistless *power*—the power of God! This side of eternity, the individual man can not sink beyond the reach of salvation. But the life of nations is governed by another law, and we see them fall, where no effort or power, even of Christianity, can recover them. Unwillingly have I been brought to the conclusion, that this is the condition of our American tribes. Their probation *as communities*, is over, their judgment day even is passed; *nationally*, they are among the lost. Let individuals, if possible, by all effort, be snatched as brands from the burning, and as trophies of the surprising grace of God—but national vitality there is none. Even if this theory is false, the Indian tribes can never be socially and politically recovered by a Gospel which teaches them to adopt and cherish the most hateful enormity of civilized life. While their teachers are slaveholders, or the defenders of slavery—while the churches to which they are invited, welcome the slaveholder to membership and communion—it is the error of one morally insane to imagine that they can be socially or politically saved. When our own civilization, the strongest and best, upon the whole, which earth ever saw, reels under the burden of slavery, and sickens with its moral poison, and gasps and struggles in its distress, what madness, what cruelty to lay all this upon the weakness of those who, in addition, have heathenism itself to contend with! We may lay aside all moral considerations, and leave out of sight the sin of slavery, and regard it only in a social and political point of view, and then safely say that slavery will present an insuperable barrier to the elevation of these tribes, and make their ruin sure.

The Indian can not endure the curse of slavery with as little injury as the Anglo-Saxon. The characteristics of the latter are activity and energy, *power* in *action;* and this tends to secure the full exercise, the complete development of his faculties. He will not rust in sloth, though surrounded with slaves, to do his bidding. He has a mental vitality which "*dies hard,*" even when throttled by slavery. He will, if possible, abandon manual labor; he will scorn all handicrafts and mechanic arts; he will suffer his home, plantation and all about him, to wear the aspect of the most helpless shiftlessness, lacking all neatness, and real comfort, but he will not lie down and doze his life away like a gorged ox, in the shade, or a pig in the stye. If he can be nothing else, he will become a politician, and busy himself in saving the Union. For such an individual, or people, slavery will not prove suddenly fatal. Though sure to destroy in the end, the strength of the character is slowly undermined.

But the Indian is naturally indolent, cruel, and sensual. The development of his nature requires the full power of all the stimulants of a free, Christian society, to cherish the weak points in his character, with a vigorous culture.

Slavery seizes upon the very worst, most odious features of his nature, and gives them supreme control of his life. His indolence; his aversion to any effort beyond the necessity of the hour; his improvidence, cruelty, and sensuality, are made all the stronger by this facility of indulgence, and to attempt to raise him to the dignity and excellence of Christian, civilized man, with this incubus on his soul, is to strive against the force of eternal law. A mission to the Indians which does not condemn and utterly exclude slavery, carries not with it one element of ultimate success. The most important missionary effort of the age, for the Indian, is that which proposes to plant among them free institutions—to hold up before them the example, and throw over them the influence of free and industrious communities.

The Kaws were encamped at no great distance from our lodgings, and they are worthy of a special place among the curiosities of Kansas. There were groups which those who are fond of statuary might love to study. They were the first persons I had ever met, who, to my certain knowledge, were entirely free from any patronage of slave-labor cotton. This sin could not be laid to their charge, for from crown to sole, not a shred of *anything* covered any part of the body. There were children of perhaps six years old walking about the public street, and mingling with others, and exhibiting no more anxiety about clothing, than the pigs they played with. From this lowest starting point of total nakedness, the styles of dress rose upward in a series, whose culminating point was a partial covering of the body. Carlyle should have seen these Kaws before he wrote his "Philosophy of Clothes;" he would have gained a tolerably clear idea how a naked Chancellor would actually appear on the wool-sack. The style next to entire nudity, was a change so slight as not to startle or offend by its abruptness. It was worn by boys of from twelve to fifteen years old, apparently, and consisted merely of a very narrow band around the loins. The next style exhibited leggins, only, with nothing above the waist. Next came one who had adopted what may be called the intermediate or half-way style, between nothing and full costume. He wore a blanket round his shoulders, but one leg of his pantaloons was missing; yet being a man of middle age he wore the *one leg* with great gravity, and, for aught I know, it might have been an *official* garb. The full dress consisted of leggins and a blanket, with no shirt; and as the weather was warm they were, generally, when sitting, naked to the waist.

The heads of the men were shaved so as to leave an upright crest about two inches high, shaped like a double cock's comb. In the center of this the scalping-lock is permitted to grow long, and is braided like a *queue*. In their poverty, ornaments were few and grotesque. The feathers of prairie hawks and eagles were worn, not ungracefully, in the hair.

All kinds and shapes of bright things were hung in the ears, of which bunches of silver drops seemed to be most highly prized, and one, a little ambitious and particular in the general style of his dress, had several strings of beads around his neck, fastened in front in some way, by a large clam-shell. The edges of the ears were colored with red paint, and a red line was frequently drawn round the base of the circular crest of hair, and sometimes the cheeks, also, were tinged. One old man, apparently from the want of means, for the purchase of paint, had mixed up some prairie mud, and daubed his face into a considerable degree of fashion and respectability.

One thing was highly amusing, and perhaps ought to be instructive. Whether naked or clothed, whether their pantaloons had two legs, or only one, whether they had paint or mud on their faces, they demeaned themselves with a gravity which nothing could disturb, and their carriage was, in general, erect, dignified, and proud; sometimes, even scornful. The only instances where I observed any relaxation of haughtiness, were where one endeavored to persuade us to break open a closet, in the house where we were staying, in order to get him some tobacco, and another undertook to sell me a coat and pantaloons, which he had probably stolen elsewhere—this last smiled, exhibited, and persuaded like an old clothes-man. On Sunday evening there was loud riot and revelry in their camps, and all seemed to join in yelling out a song, which was so softened and modulated by floating half a mile, as to enable Mr. Mason to write down its principal notes, and after his return he performed or imitated it on the organ, much to the *astonishment* and amusement of those who heard.

After all, the predominant feeling was pity for those poor creatures, ignorant, degraded, and almost friendless; apparently forsaken of God, and certainly despised and abused by man. They will soon be compelled by Government to treat for their lands, and retire before the white man.

CHAPTER XVIII.

NUMBER OF INHABITANTS NOW IN THE TERRITORY—SLAVEHOLDERS—THEIR FEELINGS AND PLANS.

We made many endeavors to ascertain this, but could arrive at no very satisfactory result. We know not how it can be determined until the census is taken. Major Ogden, at Fort Leavenworth, estimates the number on the Delaware lands alone, at twelve hundred. The more general opinion seemed to be, that there may be now (Sept. 1854), in all, some four to five thousand in the Territory. Still, this is a mere estimate.

Fictitious claims are made on all sides, and little can be known of the true state of things. The statements of some slaveholders would indicate that the whole country, or nearly so, is already occupied by friends of "the institution." A few will combine for speculation in a certain locality, and soon a squatter association is formed; a registrar and other officers are chosen from among themselves; the surrounding region is claimed; entries are made on the registrar's book, of long lists of names, and *strangers* are informed, unless they are of the "*right kind,*" that the land in that vicinity is all "*taken* up." Such combinations have been entered into sometimes, for the purpose of keeping out "the abolitionists," and if they who use this weapon should find that it has two edges, with one turned toward themselves, they need not be surprised. Such associations have "*got up*" settlers' meetings, and sent forth terrible resolutions, as the voice of the sovereigns of Kansas, of the passing of which, these said sovereigns were entirely ignorant. They have been quietly engaged in their pursuits, while a few speculators and politicians have been passing resolutions, saving the Union, and protecting and extending "our *peculiar institutions.*"

The first excitement on the borders of Missouri, in reference to the settlement of Kansas, and which manifested itself in a few meetings and intemperate resolutions, has already passed, to return no more. The actors in these scenes are even now, by no means, proud of their doings, while by the masses such proceedings are not merely discountenanced, but treated with contempt. A settler in Kansas need have no more apprehension than if he were about to locate in Illinois or Iowa.

Here and there, he will find little associations composed of those in sympathy with the slaveholders, who have, perhaps, covered the region round them with fictitious claims, in order to exclude the "Yankees" from their neighborhood, but then the same thing is also done by those who call themselves free-soilers, for the purpose of shutting out slaveholders.

This will soon be over. The different parties will, ere long, be mingled, from proximity, and the strong necessity of companionship, and of social and business relations. It is, we think, wisely and mercifully ordered in the providence of God, that extremes meet here on neutral ground.

Asperities will be softened, and prejudices removed. One little circumstance will illustrate the working of these causes.

A Missourian in the Territory, needing some assistance, applied to his own fellow Missourians, and was refused, but some New England men immediately gave him the needed aid. Not long after the Missourians invited the New Englanders to send some of their number to them, and they would show them "*good claims.*"

I have already alluded to our stay in Weston, where most of the violent proceedings, which have been published, originated; and since our return we have seen it stated, that Weston is bent on blood. We have no hesitation in saying, that no eastern man will be harmed in Weston, unless he desires to produce excitement. As the circular which we have inserted proves, the business men of that place have not participated in the folly enacted there, and which we feel sure will not be repeated, the interests of commerce demand a liberal policy, and it will be enforced.

We have seen the proceedings of a meeting held at Salt creek, in many eastern papers, which have been presented as evidence of the state of public sentiment in Kansas, and of the dangers that will there beset the path of anti-slavery, or any eastern settlers. It may, perhaps, not be amiss to give an account of this meeting, according to a Missourian who was on the ground. In the first place, the call for the meeting was so circulated, that some living within a short distance of the appointed spot, did not even hear of it until afterward. Then, the "immense multitude," mentioned in the papers, numbered not more than one hundred, assembled at one time, many of whom were Missourians, who had crossed the river to "*regulate*" the affairs of Kansas. A committee on resolutions was appointed. The majority report was in favor of liberal principles and proceedings—the minority report took the opposite and exclusive position. The author of this minority report, in spite of the ruling of the chairman, and, of course, contrary to all propriety, called for a vote on his minority report *first*, and put this vote *himself*. About seventy, including Missourians who had crossed for the purpose, voted that Kansas ought to be, and *should* be a slave State. The same man put the contrary in this form: "All who are in favor of giving up Kansas to the Abolitionists and Freesoilers, signify it," &c.

All but about thirty, then left the ground; they, appointed a new chairman, and passed the minority resolutions, *unanimously*, and then the papers spread, far and wide, the proceedings of an "immense multitude" of Kansas settlers, and the unanimity with which they determined that slavery should be established in the Territory. Such transactions exhibit the spirit and the tactics of some of the slaveholders and loud-mouthed small-politicians on the frontier. They show, plainly, what these people are capable of, and would do, were they able to accomplish their purpose—it proves the need of prompt, fearless, and united action, on the part of the friends of freedom, but it represents only the sentiments of a busy and reckless clique, to whom the business community is directly opposed.

Such meetings are merely empty gasconade, which might be followed by action, if the east should be frightened thereby.

Kansas is fully open to all who choose to make it their abode. For the present, there will be little separate cliques, or bands, drawn together by sympathies and affinities, and for a time they may keep apart, and "*claim*" and save, if they can, the country around them, for *friends*, but in a little time they will all be mingled. What is called the "free-soil" principle, is the prevailing sentiment, even in Missouri. They mean by it, however, simply this—that they are willing that all should come, and that the question of slavery should be fairly decided, by the popular vote. A "free-soiler," in western phrase, is by no means, necessarily an anti-slavery man.

From the most reliable information we could obtain, we suppose that a large majority of those now in the Territory are opposed to its becoming a slave-state. Most slaveholders, themselves, profess to consider the question as virtually settled against them, and the party of freedom have the prestige of anticipated victory.

It would, however, be a mistake, likely to be attended with fatal results, should the friends of freedom in the east relax one iota of their efforts. With all the present fair-seeming, Kansas is not yet, by any means, safe. That class is not a small one, and it will *increase*, whose final vote will be determined by circumstances, and who may be influenced at the critical moment, by those means and appliances which slaveholders, and their political abettors know so well how to employ. That anti-slavery sentiment, which is based on principle, and which can endure alike opposition or temptation, is not yet very widely spread, nor very deeply rooted in Kansas. The east and north should be aroused, until its emigrants shall be poured in by thousands, and the party of freedom is placed in an overwhelming majority, until neither a hope nor a possibility remains of making it a possession for slavery.

There are two facts by which our hopes are strengthened, that Kansas will be free, which are independent of other considerations. First, the character of the productions for which the soil is fitted, and the general nature of her resources. Her agricultural productions will be essentially those of Missouri and Kentucky, and it is exceedingly doubtful, whether, with all their prejudices in favor of the system, slavery could be now *established* in either of those States, if *that*, instead of emancipation, were the question now to be submitted to the people. As the general rule, those who will leave Virginia, Kentucky, Tennessee, and Missouri, for Kansas, are from that class who are least attached to slavery, and many of them not only have no interest in its support, but their interests stand opposed.

They are often men with large families and small means, who will emigrate for the purpose of procuring farms for their sons, and who have not the means of owning slaves, even if they had the disposition. Such men, who expect to labor themselves, will not desire the presence of the aristocratic slaveholder, who will class the free laborer with his negro servants, and treat him with contempt. It is undoubtedly true, that in Kansas are some of the finest hemp-lands in the world; but it is also true that the best of these are, for the present, embraced, in large measure, in the Indian reservations, and the question of slavery will probably be decided before these are brought into market.

Though hemp and tobacco may be successfully cultivated, and to some extent will be, yet corn, wheat, oats, and stock are likely to be the great staples of Kansas, and these are no longer a very profitable basis of slave labor, though perhaps they may be of a *slave-breeding* community. *Human cattle* may be raised in Kansas. Yet the high prices and ready market which food will command there, for years to come, will present a drawback, even upon the breeding of slaves. It is likely that horses, oxen, and mules may prove more profitable.

The second fact to which we referred is this: It seems probable that a large portion of the lands of Kansas will be "claimed" or occupied by squatters previous to the survey. As a "*claim*," or preëmption right covers but one hundred and sixty acres, it can only be by indirect methods, if at all, that larger tracts can be secured, and the watchfulness and eagerness of settlers will be likely to prevent this, in all desirable locations; so that before the lands are on sale by the Government, a large portion of them will be divided into farms of one hundred and sixty acres each, not large enough for plantations. To these considerations, it may also be added, that it would be almost a suicidal act for the slave-power to vote Kansas a slave State, against a heavy minority of freemen; and should the emigration from the north and east be carried at once so far as to constitute a considerable part, though not a majority of the population, Kansas would even then be ultimately free. Slaveholders can not live there in the presence of a strong minority of freemen. Slave property would, in the present state of feeling be almost or nearly valueless there; the emigration from the free States would, comparatively, increase, and that from the slave States decrease, and so in the end a victory will be won for freedom, if large bodies from the free States are thrown in at the very first. When once the northern States have heavy interests at stake in Kansas, those interests will be protected. Let it not be supposed that the question is finally settled, if the slaveholders of Missouri should succeed in carrying the first election. It will even then be but the beginning of a contest that in the end must be decided aright. Unless eastern emigration receives an early check, Kansas will ultimately be free. The first few thousands will draw multitudes after them.

Kansas may easily be made a free State. It is now completely in the power of freedom's friends. They can save it if they will, without unreasonable effort, and without even pecuniary sacrifice. But we desire to lift our voice in warning against the idea that it will be a free State now, as a matter of course. Every man whose circumstances will allow, should feel that he is personally called upon to go and aid in making it sure.

CHAPTER XIX.

THE IMPORTANCE OF KANSAS, AS SEEN IN HER POSITION AND RELATIONS TO OTHER PORTIONS OF THE COUNTRY.

THE eastern part of Kansas occupies the central position in that line of country which forms the eastern boundary of what is called the American Desert, a belt about two hundred and fifty miles wide, a portion of which is without timber, and almost without rains. She will then be, in an important sense, a point of departure and outfit for the western trade—an exchange point between the Eastern States and the farthest West. She will be a point of departure for the western commerce, and a point of arrival for that coming eastward from the vast regions beyond her; and should the country between Fort Riley and the Rocky mountains, become, as many suppose, mining and manufacturing regions, their supplies must be derived from the commerce and agriculture of Kansas. The position of Kansas, therefore, is certain to create for her an extensive commerce and a steady home market for all her productions.

There are, also, grave moral and political interests and influences connected with her position and relations, which render it of unspeakable importance that she should be secured from the dominion of the slave power—and that there a genuine Puritan State should be established, both as a model and center of influence, and a point of departure for other enterprises in favor of freedom. The churches of Christ and the friends of free institutions, universally, should arouse themselves to consider the significance of passing events. Are they not clear indications of the will of God? Do they not speak to us in an almost audible voice? How quickly, how completely, how unexpectedly to all, has God changed the field and character of the struggle between slavery and freedom!

Kansas may be regarded as a political upheaval. Like islands that have been formed in the night by volcanic action, or mountains suddenly lifted out of the plains of South America, Kansas has been upheaved from the political ocean, by the internal fires of party, and has become at once one of the most prominent objects on our Continent. With thousands, who a few months ago had never even heard of Kansas, it is now the chief subject of thought and inquiry. Minesota and all her northwestern sisters are partially forgotten, and the pioneer army is directing its march upon the vast central plains that form the heart of the Continent.

Rightly considered, one of the most suggestive scenes that has been looked on for a hundred years in this country, was when the first large emigrant party from New England stepped upon the slave-soil of Missouri, at St. Louis, on its way to Kansas. In that silent, unheeded act, was the inauguration of a new era, unknown though it might be to the actors themselves. It was the advance-guard of freedom's hosts which was taking possession of the lands and dominion of slavery in the name of God and humanity. It was the first ripple of that new stream of emigration which, for years to come, is to swell on that southern shore with a broader and stronger tide.

For the first time, emigration from the north has changed its direction, and turned toward the south. Should it follow along its new course with the same impetuosity and power that have marked it hitherto, then it may be safely said that a new order of things has already begun—the nature and the scene of the conflict between freedom and slavery have been changed. It is the beginning of a peaceful but irresistible occupation of southern and southwestern lands, that will roll slavery back upon itself, and remove it toward the sea-coast and the Gulf.

This change in the direction of the line of emigration may be regarded as the most interesting phenomenon at present in our country. Let once this current "*set in*" upon the south, and it will no more be checked than the flow of the Gulf-stream itself. Freedom, in its turn, will finally become aggressive, will seek extension, and conquer by an exhibition of the arts of peace. There is no clause in the Constitution to prevent northern freemen from settling *in colonies*, if they please, either in southwestern Territories or in southern States. The soil and climate invite, and the south must receive in peace this peaceful "*Army of Occupation*," though their coming will prove the overthrow of her institutions—for they will root them up in a Constitutional and Christian-like manner, by showing them a "more excellent way."

Upon the question of the settlement of Kansas, the fate of the slave-power now hangs, more especially than upon the movements of political parties. The contest for the possession of this Territory will end in giving an effectual, if not decisive blow to the defeated party. From a defeat there, slavery can never recover itself, and if the slave-power is victorious, it will have at its disposal almost every conceivable earthly advantage. It would effectually exclude the people of the northern States from the fairest and most fertile regions of the Continent, and completely hem them in with institutions at war with every principle of a free, Christian republic, and cut them off, by interposed slave States, from our Pacific possessions. But let us look for a moment at the influence which she would exert, as a free State, with institutions constructed after the Puritan model.

On the east of her lies Missouri; on the south, those Indian tribes that are just assuming some of the forms of civilization, and Texas. On these Indian lands, new Territories are soon to be erected, on the west of Arkansas. West of her is Utah.

Let us now suppose that such a State as Massachusetts, or New York, or Ohio, were established on the Territory of Kansas, and thoroughly penetrated and controlled by the spirit of freedom, and a true Christianity should there present, as a "city set on a hill," its peaceful but resistless example. It would be, for all the vast regions west and southwest of the Mississippi, even to the Rocky mountains and Mexico, the dawn of a new era, decisive of their destiny.

Such a free State as Kansas is capable of sustaining, and built on such a model, with its cities, and commerce, its capital, and manufacturing skill and power, its schools, and scientific and benevolent institutions, its churches and religious influences and observances, would wield there an influence, to which none could object, peaceful, *constitutional,* unobtrusive, but perfectly irresistible, and which, in the end, would be welcomed and rejoiced over, even by slaveholders themselves.

In this manner, without the strife of parties, without the bitterness of sectional conflict, rather by the allaying of prejudice, and the union, not severance of interests, a triumph of the noblest kind might be won over slavery—a Christian victory—the overcoming of evil with good. With the exception of a portion of its northeastern boundary, there is no mountain, lake, or river, or any other natural feature to separate it from Missouri, or any neighboring Territory, on the north, east, or south. This is a circumstance of great importance, in estimating future influences to be given and received. The Ohio river, flowing between free and slave States, is sufficient to hold them apart. Were it not for the river, these States could not be held asunder. They would soon be knit together by a thousand interlacing ties.

Except at the point just mentioned, nothing will separate Kansas from Missouri and other neighbors, but a mere boundary line, invisible to the eye, and offering no obstruction to passage. By the presence of such a State as we have supposed upon her border, and no interposing barrier, Missouri would be, perhaps slowly, but certainly revolutionized. She would be penetrated by the leaven of free institutions; she would be peacefully changed into the image

12

of the better example before her, and slavery would pass away.

In this case too, the powerful center of attraction which such a free State would form, would direct southward upon Missouri, the Territories to be formed on the south of Kansas, upon northeastern Arkansas, and western Texas, a tide of free emigration, which would prevent forever the formation of another slave State in all that region, and cut short entirely, the march of slavery in that direction.

Another consideration, bearing upon this point, should not be lost sight of. The population of Kansas will be composed of mingled elements, probably to a greater extent than any other State in the Union. It will be a neutral Territory, where for the first time in the history of the country, the tides of northern and southern emigration will meet on the large scale. Hitherto, emigration has moved westward, nearly on parallels of latitude, and these streams, except in California, have not met, though running westward on parallel lines.

The eastern States have, by emigration, *prolonged each itself westward.* We mean that this is the general result. The northern stream has now been deflected southward upon Kansas, and there the lines, from all the States, except the extreme south, will concentrate and mingle.

The emigrants from the northern States will meet there Missourians, Kentuckians, Virginians and Tennesseeans. They will be thrown into neighborhood associations. Business, social and domestic relations, will spring up between them, common interests will bind them together, prejudices will be allayed, and friendships will be established, and they will be woven together by the countless interlacings of society. If, under such circumstances, Kansas should become a free, a model State, the reflective influence which it would exert upon Missouri, Tennessee, Kentucky, and Virginia, could not be estimated.

They would then be bound to freedom and the north, by countless new ties, of the strongest and most sacred character, and the ultimate consequence would be, if a separation of the Union should ever come, it would place these States in the northern division. Rather might it be said, that such a state of things would render disunion impossible. Such results are the natural consequences of the intermingling which will take place on this "*middle ground*" of Kansas, and the flowing-forth of the affections of older communities to the new States, which their sons and their daughters have formed.

These consequences, though some of them may be remote, would be almost certain to follow from making Kansas free; they are fairly within reach of the friends of freedom now, and most earnestly do we desire that the opportunity may not pass unheeded away. We regard this idea of the colonization of the west and southwest—this conquest of slavery by the showing of the more excellent way—as one of the grandest conceptions of modern times. It is a peaceful march of freedom's armies in a holy crusade, for the securing of human rights, and the extending a true Christian civilization to our remotest borders.

It will plant northern energy, skill, capital, and industry, upon a new and nobler theater. It will move men in masses, so that their character, sentiments, and institutions, will all be preserved entire. It is not merely emigration—it is *colonization*—and these colonies, if properly formed, and wisely conducted, will settle, under God, the question of American slavery. Earnestly should the friends of freedom and a free Christianity, so exert themselves that companies may be speedily formed, all over the north, of those who will go, and of those who will embark their capital; for any company can, by judicious management, secure a rich return for capital employed. Especially do we, of Ohio, hope that southern Ohio will not hesitate to take interest and part in this great enterprise, but that she will cause herself to be represented by one of the largest and noblest colonies in Kansas. The stake which Cincinnati has in this enterprise, is a very deep one, and her business men should give it a prompt and serious consideration. Should Kansas become a slave State, the bitter and aggressive spirit of slavery would be intensified by the victory, and the late proceedings at Memphis and St. Louis, show how prompt the slave-holding power would be to exclude Cincinnati from the trade of that whole west and southwest. And they will succeed, if Kansas is linked by her institutions and sympathies to the south. Nothing has lately been presented to Cincinnati, of more importance than to bind Kansas, and all that surrounding region, to her by all the affinities which free institutions on both sides can create, and by sending there, in large numbers, the sons and daughters of Ohio, to bind Kansas to her by the ties of kindred and old association. Let it be considered, how the trade of the northern part of the great valley has thus been secured to New

York and Boston, and how those who have settled here from New Jersey and Pennsylvania, have sent back a commerce to Philadelphia.

The operation of such causes is sure, and if Cincinnati is wise, she will avail herself of them, on the large scale. No city of the Union has advantages for this work equal to hers.

CHAPTER XX.

HOMESTEAD AND PRE-EMPTION LAW.

There is no homestead law, as some have supposed, applicable to Kansas. By the law of pre-emption, any person being the "head of a family, or widow, or single man, over the age of twenty-one years, and being a citizen of the United States, or having filed his declaration of intention to become a citizen, as required by the naturalization laws," is entitled to enter upon any unoccupied public lands, and "claim" any number of acres not exceeding one hundred and sixty, (a quarter section). He must make a "*settlement*" upon the land thus claimed, and erect thereon a dwelling. This claim and settlement must be made in person, and the claimant must "inhabit and improve" the same—in order to have a *legal protection* against others who might claim the same ground.

When this land has already been surveyed, the pre-emptor must within thirty days after the settlement upon his land, "enter it," in the proper land-office, and within twelve months from the time of settlement, payment must be made. A man who makes a "claim" to unsurveyed lands, as in Kansas, must file a description of his "claim," with the Surveyor-General within three months after the survey has been made in the field, and then (though the law does not specify), it is supposed, that as in the case of surveyed lands, before stated, the settler is allowed twelve months in which to make his payment to the Government. As the survey of Kansas has not yet commenced, and little will be done until next spring, the settlers will mostly enjoy the use of their lands for perhaps two years from next spring, before payment will be required by the Government. I have thought best, however, to insert here an abstract of the pre-emption laws, prepared lately by C. C. Andrews, Esq., of Fort Leavenworth, and with special reference to the settlers in Kansas and Nebraska, and published originally in a Kansas City paper. It will be seen that a man can hold but one claim—that he must make oath that he does not claim for the purpose of selling to another or on speculation, and that no one can make a claim or "enter" land by pre-emption right who already owns three hundred and twenty acres:

LAW OF PRE-EMPTION.

MR. EDITOR:—I send you herewith, for publication, the following abridgment of the pre-emption law of 4th September, 1841, the provisions of which have been applied to the public lands in this Territory. This I do at the suggestion of some of the actual settlers; and because I believe that at the present time it is inconvenient for most of the pre-emptors in Kansas to peruse that law as readily and frequently as they might desire. The act may be found in volume V, of the United States Statutes at large, pages 453–458.

I. LANDS SUBJECT TO PRE-EMPTION.—By section ten of said act it is provided that the public lands to which the Indian title had been extinguished at the time of the settlement, and which had also been surveyed prior thereto, shall be subject to pre-emption, and purchase at the rate of one dollar and twenty-five cents per acre. And the act of 22d July, 1854, section twelve, the pre-emption of unsurveyed lands is recognized as legal. Lands of the following description are excepted: Such as are included in any reservation, by any treaty, law or proclamation of the President of the United States, or reserved for salines, or for other purposes; sections sixteen and thirty-six in each township, they being reserved for school purposes (organic act of Kansas, section thirty-four); lands included within the limits of any incorporated town, or which have been selected as the site for a city or town; lands actually settled and occupied for the purposes of trade and not agriculture; and lands on which are situated any known salines or mines.

II. The Amount designated, is any number of acres not exceeding one hundred and sixty.

III. Who may Pre-empt.—"Every person being the head of a family, or widow, or single man, over the age of twenty-one years, and being a citizen of the United States, or having filed his declaration of intention to become a citizen, as required by the naturalization laws." But no person shall be entitled to more than one pre-emptive right; and no person who is the proprietor of three hundred and twenty acres of land in any State or Territory of the United States; and no person who shall quit or abandon his residence on his own land to reside on the public land in the same State or Territory shall acquire any right of pre-emption.

IV. The Method to Perfect the Right.—The pre-emptor must make a settlement on the land in person; inhabit and improve the same, and erect thereon a dwelling. And when the land has been surveyed previous to settlement, the pre-emptor shall, within thirty days of the date of the settlement, file with the register of the proper district, a written statement describing the land settled upon, and declaring the intention of such person to claim the same under the provision of the pre-emption law. And within twelve months of the date of the settlement, such person shall make the requisite proof, affidavit and payment. When unsurveyed lands are pre-empted (act of 1854), notice of the specific tracts claimed, shall be filed with the Surveyor-General, within three months after the survey has been made in the field. And when two or more persons shall have settled on the same quarter-section, the right of pre-emption shall be in him or her who made the first settlement; and questions arising between different settlers shall be decided by the register and receiver of the district within which the land is situated, subject to an appeal and revision by the Secretary of the Treasury of the United States.

And the settler must make oath before the receiver or register that he or she has never had the benefit of any right of the pre-emption act; that he or she is not the owner of three hundred and twenty acres of land in any State or Territory of the United States, nor hath he or she settled upon and improved said land to sell the same on speculation, but in good faith to appropriate to his or her own exclusive use or benefit; and that he or she has not directly or indirectly made any agreement or contract, in any way or manner, with any person or persons whatsoever, by which the title which he or she might acquire from the Government of the United States should enure in whole or in part to the benefit of any person except himself or herself; and if any person taking such oath shall swear falsely in the premises, he or she shall be subject to all the pains and penalties of perjury and shall forfeit the money which he or she may have paid for such land, and all the right and title to the same; and any grant or conveyance which he or she may have made, except in the hands of bona fide purchasers for a valuable consideration, shall be null and void.

Proof of the requisite settlement and improvement shall be made by the pre-emptor to the satisfaction of the register and receiver, in the district in which the lands so claimed lie, who shall each be entitled to receive fifty cents from each applicant for his services rendered as aforesaid; and all assignments and transfers of the right hereby secured prior to the issuing of the patent, shall be null and void.

In the above I have sought to give all the material parts of the pre-emption act in as condensed and clear a form as practicable;

trusting it may be of service to those who wish to avail themselves of the beneficent provisions of that law.

The following letter, from the Commissioner of the land-office, may also be of service to settlers. It originally appeared in the National Era:

GENERAL LAND-OFFICE.

October 13, 1854.

SIR:—In reply to the inquiries in yours of the 10th instant, in relation to the "rights of settlers in Kansas," I have to state:

1. That a "squatter" will not be allowed to take more than one hundred and sixty acres by pre-emption.

2. That the "terms of payment" will be one dollar and twenty-five cents per acre, at any time after the survey, and *before* the commencement of the public sale, including the land settled.

3. The "putting steam saw or grist mills in operation on mill sites" will *not* give a *preference* right.

4. Payment and entry can be made after survey, and before public sale.

5. The purchase money can not be paid a portion at one time and a portion at another; nor can the pre-emptor *sell his right*, and the purchaser stand in his place.

6. The *requisites* to a pre-emption will be perceived from the accompanying copy of a circular from this office.

7. Information with regard to lands not subject to pre-emption may be obtained from this office.

8. Settlement rights before the survey, will take the precedence of school claims.

I would take occasion to remark, that none of the lands in this Territory and Nebraska, *which were ceded by the Delawares, Iowas*, and *Weas*, by *treaties in May last, are subject to pre-emption, with the exception* of the "*outlet,*" *within the Delaware cession.* The lands thus ceded (with the exception mentioned) are to be *offered at auction*, to be sold for the benefit of the Indians.

The "outlet" referred to is subject to pre-emption, because it is *excepted* from the lands to be *thus sold*, having been ceded for the specific sum of ten thousand dollars.

Respectfully, JOHN WILSON, *Commissioner*.

But the entire process of "squatting," "claiming," and settling, is not made entirely clear by this act, alone, and, therefore, some additional facts will be stated. The object of the pre-emption law should be first understood. Formerly, the "squatter" on the public lands had no protection. He might occupy a tract of public land and make upon it improvements, and then, as the public lands were sold at auction, on the day of sale, some one might overbid him, and take his and land improvements, without any means of redress on his part, unless he chose to use his rifle, as settlers sometimes did. The pre-emption law protects the actual settler in his claim to one hundred and sixty acres, and allows him to pay for it within twelve months from the time of settlement (if surveyed land), at one dollar and twenty-five cents per acre—beyond this, the Government extends no protection. But it is plainly a matter of indifference to the Government how much land a man purchases on the day of public sale, or where it is located, provided no individual makes objection. If a person, therefore, should locate himself upon ten thousand acres, more or less, in Kansas, and no other person should object, or interfere with his claim, and if on the day of public sale, after the survey, no one should bid against him, he would obtain it all at one dollar and twenty-five cents per acre. He has no *legal* security to more than one hundred and sixty acres; but then if all people are willing that he should thus hold ten thousand acres, the Government does not object to sell that quantity on the day of sale.

I have received letters inquiring, if a man should make a claim, and leave it to go for his family, whether it would be secure. There is no legal security, except to the actual settler, *residing* on the claim. But, then, if no one interferes or claims it in his absence, of course all is safe. Few men will dare "jump a claim," where it is known that there is an honest intention to settle thereon; for "*squatter*" public sentiment is strongly against such proceedings. A somewhat amusing incident, illustrating these matters, occurred at the New England settlement. A Missourian had made a claim there, and subsequently abandoned it, so that, by "squatter law," it was forfeited. A New England man then took it, and dug a well upon it, without, however, erecting any dwelling. Then the Missourian came back and resumed his claim, on the ground that the "Yankee" had no dwelling, and was not residing there; that the man who first put up his dwelling was entitled to a claim, and that he had the timber all ready for his house. The Missourian took his team and started for his timber, and when he returned with his house, the Yankee had moved a tent upon the claim—had *erected his dwelling*—and the Missourian was non-plused. Squatters make such regulations concerning these matters as please themselves. They may agree that they will allow each other to "claim" more than one hundred and sixty acres, and protect each other against intruders. They may agree that a man may have a certain time in which to bring on his family, and during that time, those who remain on the ground will protect his claim. So a man may make a claim, and hire some one to watch and protect it for him in his absence, and as has been stated, few will interfere with an honest claim; but in all this, there are no rights acquired which the Government will protect, except where an *actual settler* complies with the conditions of the law.

A "claim" is made by measuring off, as near as may be, one hundred and sixty acres, and by placing upon it a foundation of a dwelling, generally, four or eight logs, laid up as the beginning of a cabin; sometimes a line of stones is laid around a foundation; sometimes a pile of stones is laid up; and sometimes a mere stake is set up with the claimant's name thereon. All these methods are merely by sufferance, or agreement, among the squatters themselves. As the lines of the Government survey will not correspond with those of the *claims*, the claimants agree that they will mutually convey to each other, so that each shall obtain, as nearly as possible, his own.

Such rules of a Squatter Association, are here subjoined.

WHEREAS, the laws of the United States confer upon citizens the privilege of holding land by pre-emption right; and whereas the Kansas valley, in part, is now open for such settlement, or location of claims; and whereas we, the people of this convention, have, and are about to select homes in this Territory, and in order to protect the public good, and secure equal justice to all, we solemnly agree and bind ourselves to be governed by the following Ordinances:

FIRST. We recognize the right of every citizen of the United States, of lawful age, or who may be the head of a family, to select, mark, and claim, two hundred and forty acres of Land, viz: one hundred and sixty acres of prairie land, and eighty acres of timber land—and who shall, within sixty days after the treaty is ratified, proceed to erect thereon a cabin, or such other improvements as he may deem best, and shall, within sixty days after the ratification of the treaty, enter thereon as a resident.

SECOND. A claim, thus made and registered, shall be good sixty days from the ratification of the treaty, at which time the claimant, if the head of a family, shall move upon and make his home, on either the prairie or timber land, which shall make them both good, and shall be regarded so by the settlers. Single persons, or females, making claims, shall be entitled to hold them by becoming residents of the Territory, whether upon their claims or otherwise. Any person making a claim, as above, shall be entitled to a day additional, for every five miles they have to travel to reach their families.

THIRD. No person shall hold more than one claim, directly or indirectly.

FOURTH. No one shall be allowed to enter upon any previously made claim.

FIFTH. All persons failing to commence improving, or entering thereon, within the time specified, shall forfeit the same, and it shall be lawful for any other citizen to enter thereon.

SIXTH. Each claimant shall, at all reasonable times, hold himself in readiness to point out the extent of his claim, to any person who may wish to ascertain that fact.

SEVENTH. It shall be the duty of the Register to put every applicant upon proof, oath, or affirmation, that the claim offered for registry is free from the claim of any other person.

EIGHTH. Every application for registry, shall be made in the following form, viz: "I apply for certificate of registry for a claim selected and marked on the — day of — 185 , lying and being in —— containing one hundred and sixty acres prairie land, and eighty acres of timber land, and declare upon honor, that the said claim was selected and marked on the — day of — and that I am claiming but the one in my own right, and that it was not claimed by any other person, or selected;" to be signed by the applicant. Any person failing to make this certificate shall not be entitled to register.

NINTH. We agree, on the survey of the Territory, to mutually deed and re-deed to each other, so as to leave the land, as near as possible, as claimed.

CHAPTER XXI.

INDIAN LANDS AND RESERVATIONS.

The Indian lands now form but an inconsiderable portion of the Territory in quantity, but they embrace some of the most desirable parts of the country, and in particular, a large proportion of the timber on the Kansas river, and on the mouths of its tributaries. The disadvantages of the present arrangement are such, that some modification of these treaties, or the purchase of these lands entire, will soon be demanded at the hands of the Government.

In fact, we consider it impossible that these lands should long be held by the Indian tribes, as they now are. Necessity will compel a change — we only hope that it will be wisely and justly made.

At present, the Wyandots have six square miles at the mouth of the Kansas, and between that river and the Missouri; and on this tract is the only good town site, at the mouth of the Kansas, that is not in slave territory.

Then, on the north side of the Kansas, the Delawares have reserved a tract extending west from the Wyandots, forty miles along the river, and ten miles wide. The value of this reservation, and its importance to the country, will be seen when it is considered that it includes all the bottom and timber on the Kansas, and on all its tributaries for ten miles back, on the north side of the Kansas.

West of this Delaware reservation, there is next an opening of thirteen miles, between it and the lands of the Pottawatomies. Then, west of this, is the Pottawatomie tract, thirty miles long, and fourteen miles wide, on the north side of the Kansas, and four miles wide upon the south side. All west and north of this is open for settlement. On the south side of the Kansas, the Shawnee reservation begins, about four miles from the Missouri, and runs westward forty miles, and ten miles wide. For eighty miles then from the mouth of the Kansas, the bottom lands and the timber on the Kansas and its tributaries back for ten miles, are in the hands of the Indians.

It is supposed, however, that the Pottawatomies are now ready to sell, and that a treaty will be concluded the present autumn. Such a treaty would be of immense importance to the Territory. The Kansas, or Kaws, have a small tract in the neighborhood of Council Grove, which, it is said, will soon be ceded, and that all or nearly all the southeastern district will be open for settlement during the coming winter. We have no official information on these points, but well known circumstances would seem to indicate the truth of the statements.

The Osages and Ottawas, the Sacs and Kansas, have some reservations on the head waters of the Osage and Neosho rivers, and embracing some of the finest bottom lands and timber on these streams.

The Iowas have also some inconsiderable reservations in the northern district of Kansas. There is some dispute in regard to the lands lately ceded by the Delawares. The treaty was formed, it would seem, with the intention of excluding the right of pre-emption, and of bringing the lands into market, at a public sale, unshackled by "squatter" claims. The Attorney-General has decided, that this is the meaning of the treaty; that the lands are not subject to pre-emption, and that it is the duty of the Government to exclude the settlers.

At the time of our visit, in September, it was computed that there were twelve hundred settlers already on these Delaware lands, and how the Government can induce them or compel them to leave, is a question not easily answered. It is said by those best acquainted with the subject, that portions of these lands would readily sell at auction for fifty or sixty dollars per acre, if unincumbered with claims, but the settlers will combine to keep them all down to Government price, and we see not why they will not succeed.

Lawyers are already publishing opinions opposed to that of the Attorney-General, and before any final action can be had, the whole country will not only be claimed, but occupied. And in spite of treaties, we doubt not, it will be held.

So far as the great ends of civilization and Christianity are concerned, the most of these Indian lands are so occupied by the tribes as to be useless to the world, or rather they are obstacles in the progress of the country. Of this any candid observer will be at once convinced, by passing through the Territory. Among the Delawares, Shawnees and Pottawatomies are some whom civilization and Christianity have reached, but this is not true of the mass, and we fear will never be.

How their Territory is, without injustice to them, to pass into the possession of the whites, is a question we can not answer, and yet we can not doubt that the transfer will erelong be made.

CHAPTER XXII.

MULES—TECUMSEH—PROSPECTING—THE NEW ENGLAND SETTLEMENT—A MULE CHASE.

Before my visit to Kansas, I had held mules in very light esteem. I regarded them as of much lower "*caste*" than horses, and had associated them mainly with obstinacy and thistles. But I found that in Kansas, a mule was in some sort a Government officer, or, at anyrate, he was in the *employ* of the Government, and drew his rations of Government provender, and being, for aught I could discover, on the same level with some other *employees*, who have nothing to recommend them, except that they are fed by the Government, I felt a growing respect for a mule. Many of these, in the employ of Government, are exceedingly fine animals, and command high prices. They are really more serviceable than horses, are able to endure more hardship, and with less food and care, while they will also travel farther in a day. A Government mule must probably be admitted to hold a higher social rank than a common horse.

While at the Pottawatomie Mission, one of our horses was taken ill, and we were unable to proceed. We were about thirty-five miles from the New England settlement, near the mouth of the Waukereusa, and two of our party concluded to visit that spot while our horse was recovering his strength. By the kindness of a merchant, trading there with the Indians, we were furnished with a light wagon and a mule whose name was John. John, when required, however, was at large, in a pasture which reached without a fence, from the Missouri river to the Rocky mountains, and it was quite problematical in what quarter of the Mississippi valley he might be on that particular morning.

He was found, however, captured by guile, and brought in about 11 o'clock, and we started across the prairie. John was really a noble road animal. With almost no perceptible effort, with no appearance of fatigue he swept over the plains at about six miles per hour. Yet John's master was not entirely divested of the old idea that a mule is of low "caste," a mere menial, for whom kindness and mercy would be as much out of place as for any other slave. I once heard of a man excusing himself for abusing a *black* horse by saying that "he was nothing but an old nigger, anyhow," and the owner of poor John seemed to think he was "nothing but a mule, anyhow," for when I inquired how he was to be fed during this drive of thirty-five miles, he replied that I might let him pick a little prairie-grass, but it wouldn't matter if he had nothing at all. He gave us some twenty-five feet of rope with which to "*picket*" him out at night, and I asked what could be done if he should entangle himself and be cast down? he said, "let him lie till he gets up, it won't hurt him." John "was but a mule, anyhow," yet he took us faithfully, and speedily on, about fifteen miles, to Tecumseh or Stinson's, where on the south bank of the Kansas, and apparently in a healthy location, the town of Tecumseh has been laid out. The enterprise is said to be under pro-slavery influences, and that these have their center in one of the Missionaries of the Territory, and that it has been started as a rival of the New England town. In such a contest, it will probably be found necessary to enlist the energies of freemen, and the interests and necessities of trade will soon dispose of mere pro-slavery schemes.

There is a fine farming country about it, which is still mostly owned by the Indians. Mr. Stinson obtains eight hundred acres of land, through his Indian wife and children, and on this tract, as we understood, Tecumseh is located. The whole peninsula between the Waukereusa and the Kansas, is a very beautiful region, capable of supporting a dense population, from its agricultural resources alone; but in addition to this, it will probably be covered with manufacturing establishments, on account of its mineral treasures, especially iron and coal. There seems nothing to prevent this from becoming an eminently populous and prosperous region.

Just beyond Tecumseh we met a wagon, in which were five men, beside the driver, seated flat on the bottom boards. They did not appear to be a "moving" party, having no household effects with them, and we were curious to know the object of such a company abroad on the prairie. We found that they were from Illinois; that the five had hired the team as a stage-coach, or rather perhaps private carriage, and were out "prospecting" through Kansas. We afterward found a similar party who had camped out on the prairie, and whose driver, having drank himself drunk, had lost his horses in the night, and in the morning the whole party found themselves "*becalmed*" on the prairie-ocean, and not a sail in sight. Having missed what is called Big Spring, and where we were directed to slake the thirst of John, and anxious to comfort the poor animal, we halted at a log-cabin, and made known our wants. The woman was anxious to aid us, and there was a spring near by, but she had no pail, or "bucket," or vessel which would answer the purpose. At last she bethought herself of her large brass kettle, and with that we managed to "water" the thirsty John.

A few miles beyond, we reached the house of a friend, whose "Letters from Kansas" have attracted some attention through the papers. We called, and found only his lady at home. She was from Ohio, and had been accustomed to the comforts and refinements of eastern life. Amid the very manifest lack of many things which we are accustomed to class among necessaries, I expected to find her somewhat dispirited. Far otherwise. She expressed herself as "perfectly delighted." I looked around, curious to know how many of what we call comforts and necessaries, might be dispensed with, and still leave one "perfectly delighted." I found that it was not necessary to happiness that a house should have a floor, or any door, or a window, or even a roof, for our friend's house had none of these, usually considered very convenient, if not necessary appendages to a dwelling. Some poles were laid across the upright walls at one corner, on these prairie-grass was laid, and under this canopy was the bed. Under another similar canopy stood a chest of drawers and household utensils. Here then was the house of a Kansas pioneer, where a woman, fresh from the comforts and luxuries of cultivated life, cheerfully and heroically adapted herself to circumstances, and aided with a strong heart, to lay the foundations of their domestic kingdom. She could invite us to stop within her walls, but not beneath her roof. Those who sow thus in hope, will, by God's blessing, reap, in the end, with joy.

Just before sunset we reached the "Yankee settlement." A few tents were pitched on the high ground overlooking the Kansas and Waukereusa valleys, others were scattered over the level bottoms below, but not a dwelling beside was to be seen. It was a city of tents alone. We were cordially received by the intelligent and active agent, Dr. Robinson, from whom we learned, with much satisfaction, the plans and expectations of the Company. This town, where at this time (November 16), there are already six hundred heads of families, is beautifully situated on the peninsula formed by the junction of the Waukereusa with the Kansas. At the point of confluence the ground is low, and for some distance back it is a level bottom. It then rises to a second terrace, which, at the site of the town, runs quite up to the Kansas' bank. On this it is expected that the business part of the town will be located. Above, on the high, broad plateau, is the site for dwellings and public buildings. It would be difficult to find another spot combining a greater variety of attractive features than this. It is vain to describe what it was, or now is, for before these sheets can be printed it will have made many onward steps. Capital, skill, and eastern enterprise and industry, will build there, in a few months, a large town, with most of the comforts and advantages of older communities. A church has lately been organized, schools are in progress, a newspaper is printed there, and nearly a thousand souls are already collected, and a college even is now in prospect.

We had a comfortable night's rest in Dr. Robinson's tent, and in the morning were introduced to the only "boarding house on the hill." Two very intelligent ladies, from Massachusetts, had united their forces and interests, and had taken "boarders." In the open air, on some logs of wood, two rough boards were laid across for a table, and on wash tubs, and kegs, and blocks, they and their boarders were seated round it. This was the first boarding-house in the new city of Lawrence. All were cheerful, hopeful and full of energy, and the scene reminded me of Plymouth Rock. Would that there might be found there the same depth of piety, the same sublimity of faith and loftiness of aim!

We had "picketed out" John over night, and in the morning he was missing, having pulled up his stake and decamped. We took a hasty look over the prairie from the eminence, but he could not be descried. Dr. Robinson's horse, a large and powerful animal, was saddled by his tent, and he urged me to take him and go in search. I soon heard of John, who, at a distance of some two miles, was making his way homeward, as was said, "at a sweeping trot." By hard riding, I came at length in sight, and here his speed and sagacity were at once made manifest. I supposed that a horse, of course, could overtake a mule; but with the full speed of the horse, I could barely come up with him, and then was entirely unable to seize his rope, which he was trailing. Once I headed him, but when I wheeled, he passed me by a skillful dodge, and went straight on. We were now some four miles away, and the prospect of capture was small. I changed my plan, and took a wide sweep out into the prairie. John was evidently gulled by this stratagem; he halted and began to feed. I came into the road far ahead, and gathering to my aid three men, who were at a cabin, we held a council. John's suspicions were again aroused, and he was once more moving homeward. Two of the men took a long rope, and stretching it across the road, let it rest on the ground, while one stood at each end, ready to jerk it up and catch him, as he passed between them. On he came, apparently unconscious, but just as we thought him safe, he fathomed the scheme, and slipped skillfully round the rope; but luckily, as he trailed his own "*lariat*" past, it came within reach and was seized. But John could easily *tow* one man, and forward still he went, pressing toward home. He was gaining in speed, so that the man could scarcely keep his feet, when another also seized the rope; but still the mule went on. At last, after a doubtful struggle, by a change in the line of draught, they took a sidewise purchase on his neck, and slowly *rounded him in.* He submitted himself with all meekness, evidently considering that he was a lawful prey. Taking a turn of the "lariat" round the horn of the saddle, I started the Doctor's powerful gray, expecting that the mule would quietly follow. The "lariat" round his neck was about twenty-five feet long, and the moment the "*slack*" was taken up, it was found that John had cast anchor. When he found that the direction I had taken was not homeward, he became suddenly stiff and motionless, as if smitten with catalepsy. It now became doubtful which of several possible things would actually occur; whether the strength of my "gallant gray" would fail, or the saddle girths would give way, or the mule's neck would be broken, or his obstinacy would be overcome. The chances for each were about equal, and my resolution having been a little strengthened by the exciting chase, I urged gray sharply forward. I shall never forget the expression of John's countenance and general aspect, when he "felt the halter draw." He seemed not to be angry or revengeful, but closing his eyes, as if perfectly resigned, and forgiving his enemies, he would meet his fate in a manner becoming a mule. Gray was a very tall and very powerful animal, and accustomed to a long and steady pull. Slowly John seemed to be "drawn out," until it was nearly a straight line from the top of his nose to the root of his tail, yet his feet were all immovable. He seemed "planted out" in the prairie. But the great hight of the horse put him at great disadvantage, for the line of draught was so high, that it raised him gradually from his fore-feet, and at last, with a forward leap, like a kangaroo, he started. Gray, proud of his victory, put himself into a gallop, and John, with his obstinacy dreadfully stretched, if not entirely broken, was hastened back to the camp.

When returning, we were obliged to trust entirely to the sagacity of this animal, having lost our way in the prairie. Left to himself, he turned off at right angles to the road we were following, and taking the open prairie, pursued what proved to be an air-line route to the Mission.

CHAPTER XXIII.

THE MOUNDS — AN INDIAN MURDERER — INTERESTING CUSTOM.

The mounds of the prairies are among the most interesting features in the scene, and probably no other objects in the Mississippi valley have given rise to so many conjectures as they. The large mounds of Kansas present the appearance of artificial structures, and especially when seen from a distance, rising out of the plain like immense flattened cones. Indeed, the general outline of the prairie, when seen against the sky, as well as that of the bolder bluffs and mounds, seems as if shaped by human art, such is the regularity of the form. This, however, is especially true of the mounds. They are so perfectly rounded, that it seems impossible that the result should have been produced by any natural phenomena. Many of the smaller mound-shaped structures of the west have, doubtless, been reared or modeled by the hand of man, but it seems strange that any one should mistake such elevations as the large mounds of Kansas for artificial structures. A single glance at their formation, shows it to be identical with that of the neighboring elevations; the rock strata lying as regularly in them as in any of the bluffs of the river. That they have been upheaved there by the hand of God and not man, is a fact beyond all question.

Still, some of them at least, stand precisely where it would seem they might have been wanted, in certain styles of defense or warfare, and even in modern war, a battery placed on their tops would command the whole country, on every side, within range of the guns, while to storm such a battery would be a serious work. I see no objection to the idea that they may have been used for military or religious purposes, and were partially shaped for such purpose by the labor of man. The regularity of their outline seems to favor this opinion, though it is by no means a necessary inference. Doubtless, in our attempts to "re-people the past," we may believe that these mounds have been used for posts of military observation, or for the kindling of beacon fires, or for "high places" of worship and sacrifice, or even under such heavens, for astronomical observations. For all such purposes, they are certainly suitable, and for such uses, or even for a pleasure resort in these level regions, they may have had their natural inequalities smoothed away. But they belong to the hills, and not to the works of man; and we hope that human folly will never dig them down, or deface them in any way. Within sight of the Mission, there are two such mounds, and a story was related to us, in connection with one of them, interesting in itself, and illustrating a singular custom of the Indians.

A few years since, at the base of this mound, a chief resided, whose young daughter was a girl of uncommon beauty, and this beauty was but the external manifestation of a pure and noble spirit. As a matter of course she had many admirers among the young braves of her nation. Her nature was above the arts of a coquette; and loving one among them all, and only one, she hesitated not to let her preference be known, not only to the Young Eagle who had won her heart, but also to those whose suit she had rejected. Among the rejected suitors one alone so laid it to heart as to desire revenge. He, the Prowling Wolf, was filled with rage, and took little pains to conceal his enmity, though he manifested no desire for open violence. Both these young men were brave, both skillful in the use of weapons, which far away on the buffalo plains had sometimes been used in battle; but while Young Eagle was noble, generous in spirit, and swayed by such high impulses as a young savage may feel, the Wolf was reserved, dark and sullen; and his naturally lowering brow seemed, after the maiden had refused him, to settle into an habitual scowl. The friends of the Young Eagle feared for his safety. He, however, was too happy in the smiles of his chosen bride to trouble himself concerning the enmity of another, especially when he knew himself to be his equal both in strength and skill.

The Indian customs did not permit the young couple to be much alone with each other, but they sometimes contrived to meet at twilight on the top of this mound, and spend there together a happy hour. Young Eagle was a favorite with his tribe, except among the kinsmen of the Wolf; and among the whites too, he had made many friends, one of whom, who had hunted much with the Eagle, had given him a Colt's revolver, the only one owned in the tribe. Delighted with this formidable weapon, he had made it a plaything till he became skillful in its use, and always wore it about him in addition to his other arms. This was a second cause of enmity which the Wolf laid up in his heart. He seemed to be revolving some dark scheme; but his secret, if he had one, was confided to no one. Bitter words sometimes were passed between the young warriors, but nothing more; yet it was felt that at any time a sudden rousing of passion might end in bloodshed.

One summer evening, just as the moon was up, Young Eagle sought the top of the mound for the purpose of meeting his future bride, for their marriage was agreed upon, and the appointed day was near. One side of this mound is naked rock, which for thirty feet or more is almost perpendicular. Just on the edge of this precipice is a footpath, and by it a large flat sandstone rock forms a convenient seat for those who would survey the valley, while a few low bushes are scattered over a part of the crest of the mound. On this rock Young Eagle sat him down to await the maiden's coming. In a few moments the bushes rustled near him, and rising, as he thought, to meet her, a tomahawk flashed by his head, and the next instant he was in the arms of a strong man and forced to the brink of the precipice. The eyes of the two met in the moonlight, and each knew then that the struggle was for life. Pinioned as his arms were by the other's grasp, the Eagle frustrated the first effort of his foe, and then a desperate wrestle, a death-wrestle, followed, in which each was thoroughly maddened. The grasp of the Wolf was broken, and each instantly grasping his adversary by the throat with the left hand, sought his weapon with the right—the one his knife, the other his revolver. In the struggle the handle of the knife of the

Wolf had been turned in the girdle, and missing it at the first grasp, ere he could recover himself the revolver was at his breast and a bullet through his heart. One flash of hatred from the closing eye, and the arm of the dying warrior relaxed; and as the body sank the Eagle hurled it over the precipice, and in his wrath fired bullet after bullet into the corpse as it rolled heavily down; and this not satisfying his revenge, he ran round and down the side of the mound, and tore off the scalp of his foe.

The young girl, who was ascending the mound to meet her lover, heard these successive shots, and knowing well from what source such rapid discharges alone could come, hastened on, and came just in season to see the Eagle scalping his victim. She soon brought her family to the spot, and every circumstance of the transaction showed at once the dangerous position in which the Eagle was placed. There was no witness of the combat, no means whatever of showing that he had smitten the Wolf in self-defense. The number of ball-holes in the body, and the tearing off of the scalp, all seemed to bear evidence against him, and he knew that the friends of the Wolf would take advantage of every circumstance in order to procure his death as a murderer. He felt that death was certain if he submitted himself for trial, and he therefore determined to defend himself as best he might, and await the result, as his only chance for life.

These Indians observe the law that was established among oriental nations long before the time of Moses, by which the shedding of blood may be rightfully avenged by the nearest kinsman of the slain, while the murderer, in this respect an outlaw, will of course defend himself as best he may.

At the same time the friends of the deceased are at liberty to accept a ransom for the life of their friend, and often—if for a time the murderer escapes the blow of the avenger of blood—a compromise is effected, and the affair is settled. In the meantime the avenger of blood assumes the office at the risk of his own life, for if he falls, retribution is not demanded for him, but the next of kin takes up the original demand only for the blood of the first one slain.

The Young Eagle at once took his resolution, sustained by the advice of his friends. Completely armed he took possession of the top of the mound, which was so shaped that while he was himself concealed, no one could approach him by day without being exposed to his fire—and he had two devoted and skillful allies, which, together with his position, rendered him far more than a match for his single adversary, the avenger of blood—the brother of the Wolf. These allies were his bride and a large sagacious hound which had long been his hunting companion, and had guarded him many a night when camping on the prairies. The girl had in her veins the blood of Indian heroes, and she quailed not. She demanded with lofty enthusiasm to be made his wife, and then, acquainted with every stratagem of savage war, and with every faculty sharpened by affection, and her husband's danger, she watched, and warned, and shielded him with every art that the roused spirit could suggest, and which could be safely practiced.

In vain the brother of the Wolf surveyed from afar this fortress of the Eagle. It was evident that long before he could reach a point from which the young warrior could be seen, he would himself be within the range of his rifle without a cover of any kind. Often, by night, he attempted to ascend the mound, but scarcely could he put his foot upon its base before the dog of the Eagle would give his master the alarm, and then to approach would be only to go to his death. It was no mystery how the Eagle was supplied with food, for the young wife showed no solicitude, and yet no one saw her form, or heard her footsteps on the mound.

The brother of the Wolf knew well that the Eagle's wife must supply him with food, and determined, if possible, to entrap him. He therefore studied and imitated her gait, he obtained opportunities of observing her dress, and when he felt that he was perfect in his part, he arrayed himself one evening in a dress the exact counterpart of hers, with knife and tomahawk concealed beneath, and bearing some food openly before him, took, just at twilight, the common path up the mound, where he knew the mere sound of footsteps would be less likely to alarm the dog or his master, and he hoped to approach so near without suspicion, that he might, by a sudden rush, secure his victim. His plan was skillfully executed. He imitated well the light step of Eagle's wife; the approaching form was one familiar to the dog, and he had not caught the scent. He wagged his tail as he lay with his eye fixed as if he would soon bound up and forward with a welcome. The Eagle addressed his supposed wife in gentle tones and bade her hasten. The blood avenger was within ten feet of his intended victim, and thought that all was gained, when the dog, with one yell and one bound, threw himself upon him and bore him to the earth, with his jaws grappled to his throat. Entangled by the female dress and throttled by the hound, he could not draw his knife, and the Eagle, who comprehended the scene at a glance, deprived him of his weapons, while held by his dog, and then pinioned his arms. "Now go to your friends," said the young warrior, "I crave not your blood. Your brother sought my life, on this very spot, and I slew him, but only to save my own. But stay; you shall go home as a warrior should. You have shown some skill in this." He cut the pinions from his arms and gave him back his weapons. They were taken in silence and the humbled, yet grateful foe withdrew.

Three months thus had passed away, and negotiations were opened for a ransom. The friends in such a case agree first to treat, but do not engage to accept what may be offered for life. This is to be decided only on a spot appointed for the ceremony, and with the shedder of blood unarmed, and completely in their power, and bound by the law, to make no resistance. When the parties are present, and the proposed ransom is offered, it is considered by the friends of the slain man, and if accepted, all is settled; but if not they have the right to slay the murderer on the spot, without resistance from him or from his friends.

In this case the friends of the Wolf agreed to consider a ransom, and Young Eagle consented to abide the issue, he and his friends hoping that the sparing of the brother's life might have some influence in the decision, and beside it was now generally believed in the tribe that the Wolf had been the aggressor.

At the day appointed the parties met in an open space with hundreds to witness the scene around. The Eagle, all unarmed, was first seated on the ground, then by his side was laid down a large knife with which he was to be slain, if the ransom was not accepted. By his side sat his wife, her hand clasped in his, while the eyes even of old men were dim with tears. Over against them, and so near that the fatal knife could be easily seized, stood the family of the slain Wolf, the father at the head, by whom the question of life or death was to be settled. He seemed deeply moved, and sad, rather than revengeful. A red blanket was now produced and spread upon the ground. It signified that blood had been shed which was not yet washed away, the crimson stain remaining. Next a blanket all of blue was spread over the red one. It expressed the hope that the blood might be washed out in heaven and remembered no more, and last, a blanket purely white was spread over all, significant of a desire that nowhere on earth or in heaven a stain of the blood should remain, and that everywhere, and by all, it should be forgiven and forgotten.

These blankets, thus spread out, were to receive the ransom. The friends of Eagle brought goods of various kinds and piled them high before the father of the slain. He considered them a moment in silence and then turned his eye to the fatal knife. The wife of the Eagle threw her arms around her husband's neck, and turned her eyes imploringly full on the old man's face, without a word. He had stretched his hand toward the knife when he met that look. He paused; his fingers moved convulsively, but they did not grasp the handle. His lips quivered, and then a tear was in his eye. "Father," said the brother, "he spared my life." The old man turned away. "I accept the ransom," he said, "the blood of my son is washed away. I see no stain now on the hand of the Eagle, and he shall be in the place of my son.

The feud was completely healed. All were at last convinced that the Eagle was not a murderer; the ransom itself was presented to his wife as a gift, and he and the "avenger of blood" lived afterward as friends and brothers.

CHAPTER XXIV.

AN INTERESTING FAMILY—HUNTING ON THE PLAINS AND AMONG THE ROCKY MOUNTAINS—WINTER ADVENTURES ON THE PRAIRIES.

In our journey homeward, from Council Grove, we found ourselves, one evening at twilight, in sight of a solitary log-cabin. It was new, and had a most substantial look, quite superior to the common "shanty." For this reason, and one much stronger still, viz: that there was not another dwelling nearer than twelve miles, we requested the privilege of stopping for the night. The proprietor, a hearty, robust-looking man, with an open frank countenance, and prompt, decided air, gave us to understand that he intended his establishment for the accommodation of travelers, and we at once felt very much at ease "in our inn." The house was in the most approved style of Kansas architecture, having two rooms on the floor and an open passage between. Back of the house we saw a brightly-blazing fire, and as the evening was somewhat cool, we sat down in its cheerful glow. The spot proved to be the kitchen. A fireplace had been formed by piling the turf of the prairie in a semicircle of about eight feet in diameter, and within this, shielded thus partly from the wind, was a huge wood fire, that sent its red glare far over the prairie. Rough boards laid upon poles formed a partial covering, and a range of shelves held the common utensils for cooking. Amid this rudeness, however, there were some things that appeared a little out of place in Kansas, judging from what we had already seen, a few features or indications of a more civilized life than we had latterly met, especially in the cooking department, and we began to be curious to know something of our host. There were no females about the house. A slender, pale-faced, young man, was busy over the fire with different dishes for the supper.

We had, during the afternoon, captured a prairie-hen, which we desired for supper, and one of our number sat down to pick and dress it: our host coming up at the time, observed that we seemed not to understand those birds, and taking it himself, he almost in an instant stripped off its skin, instead of picking off its feathers, and in a moment more the bird was ready for cooking

Some fresh fish were produced, just caught in a stream close at hand, and the manner in which our host gave direction to his cook, or aided, himself, in the work, showed that he was quite familiar with an art so interesting to us just then.

The third member of this family, was a young man, apparently about twenty-eight years old, with a fine form and manly features, in the garb of a common laborer, but with a demeanor somewhat above his style of dress. The pale-faced young cook was, we found, a Mormon, who having come thus far with a band of these "latter day saints," had been detained by the sickness of his wife. Here she died, and here he had since remained. He was an Englishman, and thus far this land of promise had been one of sorrow, and disappointment, and poverty, and these had written a history on his form and face. Our host, as he informed us in the course of the evening, was born in the northeastern part of New England, had left his father's house, when young, to indulge a desire for roving, and had spent, thus far, a rover's life. A portion of this life had been spent on the ocean; a part in South America; a part in Mobile and New Orleans; a part in New York; a part on the plains of Kansas and Nebraska, and among the Rocky mountains—and last of all, having been persecuted for anti-slavery sentiments in a town of western Missouri, he had left in disgust, and come over into Kansas, determined to aid in making the Territory free. The third was a young Virginian, who also tired of home, among other wanderings, had spent five years with the Indians, on the western plains and among the Rocky mountains. To complete the group, there walked in under our shed, a tall six-footer from the Emerald isle—Patrick, of course, by name. His toes had walked out of the ends of his shoes; his "pants" were cut across at the knees; he had neither coat nor vest, but, instead, an Indian blanket thrown over his shoulders, and a short pipe just cleared the end of his nose. England and Ireland, New England, Virginia, and Ohio, were all represented in that small company—a fit representation of the future mingled population of Kansas. Patrick explained his dilapidated state, by informing us that he and his brother had been out some weeks "prospecting," and that finally, near this point, each had located a claim, and Kansas was to be their future home. He was now on his way to St. Louis, where Judy and the children were.

Such was the interesting company that had met in the kitchen of this Kansas hotel. On the ends of the poles over head the chickens of our host were roosting—two large dogs stood by the fire, except when they ran off to bark at each new sound in the prairie, and a pet horse would occasionally come and stick his nose in the flour and salt dish, which the cook was using for supper.

After supper was over (which was really well served, through skill acquired by our host in former years), we sat down to listen to the various talk of our associates. Two of them had been connected with many a wild and stirring adventure, and from them we gained some knowledge of life on the buffalo plains and among the Rocky mountains. The Virginian had been five years among the Indians of these regions, and some of his recitals of incidents were exceedingly graphic and stirring. We inquired of him concerning the grizzly bears, and, among other things, asked him in regard to their size. "They grow," he said, "as *large as the law allows.* Some of them will weigh eighteen hundred, and if a man should see one of these critters walking up to him on his hind feet, and swinging his fore-paws, he would be apt to think he was *going to the Legislatur'* mighty quick. Even an Indian," he said, "is often terribly scared by one of these bears. We camped one evening, just at sunset, by the side of a small creek in the prairie, and a little beyond was tall prairie-grass and some small bushes. One of the younger Indians strayed over among these, looking for game. In a few moments we heard first his gun, then the war-whoop, then a yell which was prolonged to a continuous scream, then the *scared* Indian broke cover on a clean run, loping for life, and close at his heels a grizzly bear, that shuffled and shook as he ran, as if he hadn't a bone in his body. A Frenchman seized his gun and ran to meet them, and fired at the bear without stopping him; and then he too turned, and the two came on in double quick time, the bear striking and snapping at their rear. In a moment more he was in reach of all our guns, and we brought him to a dead halt. But not the poor Indian. He ran through the camp, giving the war-whoop at every leap, and went far beyond into the prairie, before he could be brought up and made to know where he was. An old hunter," he said, "is never anxious to 'scrape acquaintance' with a grizzly bear. One who knows them will not shoot at one from choice, except with at least an ounce ball, and when he feels entirely certain of a dead shot. The hunters are willing to give them a wide berth, unless they have greatly the advantage. I saw in the mountains," he continued, "a man whose arms and chest were stripped nearly bare of flesh, and who was covered with scars elsewhere, from a battle with one of these bears. He was a Frenchman, and he and a companion were hunting and traveling alone, and were, of course, strongly bound to each other. They met unexpectedly, one day, a grizzly bear, who at once attacked them. They both fired, and having only wounded the animal, they both turned and ran. After having gained some distance ahead, one looked back and saw that the bear had caught his companion, and that he was making desperate efforts to defend himself with his hunter's knife; while the bear was tearing his flesh in the most horrid manner. His regard for his companion overcame his love of life, and he resolved to aid him or die with him. He ran back, and as he could not wait to re-load his gun, he attacked the bear with his knife and hatchet. After a desperate conflict, in which both were dreadfully mangled, the bear fell partly upon one and died. For a long time neither was able to rise. The flesh upon the arms and chest and face of the one first overtaken by the bear was torn into strings, or stripped entirely off, so that the bones lay bare, yet no artery was cut. The other was at length able to crawl on his belly to a spring at some distance, and obtain some water for himself and his friend. For days he crawled thus back and forth for water, unable to rise upon his feet; and when their little stock of food was gone, they cut pieces from the bear and ate them raw, drinking water from the spring. Often, he told me, the wolves would come and eat on one side of the bear while we lay on the other. The one least hurt recovered so as to nurse his companion, whose frightful wounds began to heal, and in the end they were relieved by a party of trappers. The one I saw," said the Virginian, "had very little meat left on him. Better let a grizzly alone if you can't put an ounce ball through the vitals."

This same hunter gave us some interesting facts in regard to hunting on the plains. He told us that buffaloes are hunted on horseback, with horses that are trained to the chase, and that love it well. Each hunter is provided with a lasso, or "lariat" (as we found it usually called in Kansas), and a very short gun, with a barrel not more than from fourteen to eighteen inches long, and carrying an ounce ball. These horses, he said, though not large, are able to hold with the lasso from the horn of the saddle the most powerful and furious buffalo. They are so skillful, that the instant the lasso strikes the horns of the buffalo, they brace themselves away from the animal, and inclining the whole body strongly inward, and gradually running on a curving line, they soon are able to *round the buffalo in,* and expose his huge side to the hunter's shot at the distance of a few feet only. At other times the hunter rides among the herd, and loading his short gun very rapidly, is able to slay a large number in a little time. The hunter is able to indicate to his horse the very animal which he wishes to follow, and he seldom loses him, or misses him, amid all the confusion of the flying herd. The elks, he said, when they are suddenly come upon, seem unable from fright to run swiftly, but rather leap up and down than run, and a hunter with a short gun and a fleet horse will sometimes shoot down four or five before they are fairly under-way, but when at full speed they are more fleet than the horse.

Our host, who had for some time been engaged in the transportation of furs, for the Fur Company, from the Rocky mountains, gave us an account of some of his winter adventures in the far-western wilds. He started, one winter, he said, with twenty-four mules, loaded with furs, and three men beside himself, he having charge of the company. Their destination was Fort Laramie. This fort is about six hundred miles northwest of Fort Leavenworth. The snow fell deeper day by day, until the prairie was one trackless waste, through which the animals could scarcely make their way; little could be procured for them to eat, and the weather was bitterly cold. From cold, fatigue and want of food, the animals failed, one after another, and died, until when one morning they heard the drum-beat of Fort Laramie, there were only four mules alive. They started for the fort, but the snow was so deep that they were obliged to tread a path for the animals, and soon they lost all knowledge of the direction of the fort, and wandered helplessly about in the snowy waste, and at night found themselves without any shelter whatever, except what a large log could give them, breaking, a little, the sweeping blast. One of the men became benumbed with cold before they reached this place, and in spite of all efforts to rouse him and urge him on, sat down in the snow and died. To save him from the wolves, they dug a grave in a deep snow-drift, and then hurried on with what speed they could, beating a path as they went. They were soon so chilled, that as their only hope, having exhausted all their food, they cut the throat of a mule and drank the warm blood. Somewhat revived by this, they cut off some of the mule's flesh, made a meal of a part, and reserved the rest for the future. The next morning, not knowing where they were, nor what direction to take, they wandered almost despairingly on. The prairie was without a tree or bush — one limitless waste of glittering, driving snow. Ere night, however, guided by a kind Providence, they came in sight of Fort Laramie, and reached it with three mules and three men remaining. Such are some of the perils of the life of the hunter and fur-trader, and such are common scenes on our wild frontier.

With such tales the evening passed away. In the meantime, Patrick was becoming talkative, if not eloquent.

Whisky had excited his brain and loosened his tongue, and his love of liberty and patriotism swelled to overflowing. Against the Pope, and slaveholders, and the Mormons, he was especially angry, and declared himself ready to leave Judy, at any time, and shoulder his musket and bring the Mormons into subjection to United States law. After we retired, he commenced a lofty oration upon the blessings of liberty, and the greatness of America, and I fell asleep to the music of Patrick's eloquence, resounding the names of Washington and Lafayette.

CHAPTER XXV.

NEBRASKA.

After the somewhat minute descriptions which have been given of Kansas, little need be added in order to present a correct idea of Nebraska. In many important features, the Territories so nearly resemble each other, that a picture of one will present also the aspect of the other. The general appearance of the prairie is the same in both Territories, and there are the same great divisions in both, presenting a fertile agricultural district, along the Missouri; a central tract destitute of timber, sandy and poorly supplied with water; and a mountainous region west of this, comprising the Black Hills and the Rocky mountains.

A large and fertile tract, lying between the Kansas and the Platte or Nebraska, is situated partly in one Territory and partly in the other, and the description, therefore, of the northern district of Kansas, on the Nemaha, Wolf creek, and the head waters of the Big Blue and Vermilion is also a description of the remainder, which lies adjacent in Nebraska.

The prairies of the latter Territory are considered to be more "*broken*" than those of Kansas, and the proportion of waste land is also greatest in Nebraska. To describe this

Territory, in detail, would, therefore, be in the main, only a repetition of what has already been written concerning Kansas, and it will be necessary, on this account, to dwell only on some of the larger characteristics, which are peculiar to itself.

Nebraska is much larger than Kansas. It reaches through nine degrees of latitude, from the fortieth to the forty-ninth parallel, having the irregular ridge of the Rocky mountains for its western boundary, and the equally irregular line of the Missouri for its eastern frontier, until that river turns westward, near Fort Mandan. Its average breadth, therefore, can only be approximately stated, as about five hundred miles.

Assuming this to be correct, Nebraska contains about three hundred thousand square miles. Its general character may, perhaps, be understood, by tracing eastward the parallels of latitude that bound it, and observing the country which they inclose. We find, by this experiment, that its northern boundary runs eastward, north of lake Superior, north of the inhabited portions of Canada, and strikes the Atlantic at the island of New Foundland, passing through cold and inhospitable regions; while its southern boundary runs through central Illinois, central Indiana and Ohio, and southern Pennsylvania, touching the ocean in the latitude of Philadelphia. Within these limits, are embraced New England and the Canadas, New York, New Jersey, Pennsylvania, northern Ohio, Illinois and Indiana, and all of Michigan, Iowa, Wisconsin and Minesota—the most healthful regions on the continent. It will require more exact meteorological observations than have yet been made, to form a correct opinion of the climate of Nebraska, as compared with the regions that lie east of it, between the same parallels. Its elevation above the sea will, of course, largely influence its climate, which may be still farther modified by local causes, such as the position, hight and direction of its mountain ranges.

Western Iowa and western Minesota present, of course, the counterparts of the eastern portions of Nebraska, as they are divided only by the Missouri river.

Nebraska may be spoken of under six general divisions. The first is the high and fertile plateau, or "divide," between the Kansas and the Nebraska. It has already been sufficiently described, and is, probably, at least for the present, the most attractive district in the Territory. The second is the valley of the Nebraska proper. The lower portion of this valley, for about two hundred and fifty miles, westward from the Missouri river, is well watered and fertile prairie.

Up to this point there is a fair supply of timber on the Platte and its tributaries, and the country, except that it lies further north, and consequently has a colder climate, offers about the same inducements to settlers as the valley of the Kansas. The climate of the latter has more of the "sunny south," and the winters are shorter and less severe. Beyond this point, westward, the comparatively dry and sandy plains appear, which form the pasture-grounds of the buffalo, elk, deer, and antelope. This lower portion of the Nebraska valley, and the "*divide,*" mentioned as forming the southern district of the Territory, will first be occupied, both from its superior attractions, and the greater facility with which it can be approached. It seems to abound with coal, and as in Kansas, this coal is doubtless accompanied by iron.

The Nebraska river is wide and shallow, and although a small steamboat has, in time of high water, ascended it several hundred miles, it may be regarded as almost useless for the purposes of commerce, spreading out as it does into broad shallows, and divided, at times, into several streams, that often lose themselves in the sands. Voyagers, in descending the river, even with small boats, after following for days along one of these streams, will find it sinking away in the sands, and disappearing altogether, subjecting them to the labor of dragging their boat again up the stream, to explore another channel, perhaps with similar results.

Two towns are already projected near the mouth of this stream, and in the vicinity of Council Bluffs, and around and back of them the country is being filled up with settlers. Doubtless the annual flood that pours into Iowa will, hereafter, aid also in populating the opposite shores of Nebraska. The attractions of the latter are at least equal to those of Iowa.

The third division is the valley of the Missouri, from the valley of the Platte to the valley of the Yellow Stone. For this long distance, along the western bank of the Missouri, runs the fertile belt which has been described as about two hundred and fifty miles wide in Kansas and the southern division of Nebraska. Although it has not been fully explored, this belt is supposed to be narrower on the north of the valley of the Platte, than it is in southern Nebraska, and in Kansas. It is represented, moreover, as deficient in timber. These points, however, can only be settled by a more complete survey than has yet been made. It is not improbable that the supply of timber may be found more abundant than present impressions would indicate, and I am quite prepared to expect, that the skill and enterprise of American farmers will find the means of obtaining comfort and wealth in those regions, both of Kansas and Nebraska, which many are disposed to condemn as worthless. I am by no means ready to believe that large tracts, in either Territory, are to remain desert and waste, as incapable of affording the means of subsistence. It is not unlikely, that some, who represent portions of these regions as uninhabitable, would be even more ready to be discouraged at the appearance of many parts of New England.

As we approach the valley of the Yellow Stone, timber becomes more abundant, both on the Missouri and its tributaries, and westward from this point there are dense forests along the streams—and in some parts, according to Gov. Stevens, they cover the face of the country. The fourth district is the valley of the Yellow Stone. This may ultimately prove the most desirable portion of Nebraska. Although it lies in a high northern latitude, its sheltered position, between the Rocky mountains on the west and the Black Hills on the east, will probably secure it a moderate climate. It is described as presenting, not so much the aspect of a prairie land, as of an immense valley, walled in by lofty, wooded mountains, that abound in scenes of grandeur and of beauty.

The Yellow Stone rises in the Rocky mountains, and pursues a northeasterly course, of about one thousand miles, to the Missouri. It has been found navigable for barges, more than eight hundred miles from its junction with the Missouri, and several of its tributaries may, in like manner, be ascended with boats. The Yellow Stone has been ascended nearly a hundred miles by steamboats, and it is not unlikely that it may be found navigable for small steamboats, for a much greater distance. Its valley is represented, by those who have seen it, as one of the most beautiful valleys in the world—so vast in its dimensions, abounding in timber and streams of water, with a soil exceedingly fertile, and with scenery that charms with its loveliness and awes by its grandeur. The sources of the Yellow Stone are not far from those of the Columbia, and the valley of the Yellow Stone may yet have a commerce both with the Atlantic and Pacific slopes of the Continent. It is said, by hunters, that a branch of the Yellow Stone, and one of the Columbia, head in one common spring.

The valley of the Missouri, above the Yellow Stone, that of the Maria river and the valley of the Yellow Stone itself, form, together, an immense region, abundantly supplied with streams, and springs, and timber, with fertile soil and most attractive scenery. This region can even now be reached by steamboats, for the Missouri, when not frozen, is navigable, for small steamboats, to the Great Falls, many hundred miles above the Yellow Stone; and it is supposed, that boats built above the falls, may run up to the Rocky mountains. In these regions, pine, cedar and fir trees are said to abound, and when we consider the vast extent of prairie country below, it becomes a most interesting question, whether a supply of this timber can not be obtained from the upper Missouri and its tributaries.

It is not unlikely that this may be the case, and that heavy lumber establishments may erelong be built upon these upper waters. A writer, quoted in the Home Missionary Journal, and whose articles appeared originally in the New York Tribune, speaks of Nebraska as follows:

"The surface of the country, from the Missouri river westward to the spurs of the mountains, is rolling prairie, but little diversified in its aspect, save by the intersection of its streams. The soil, for a space varying from fifty to one hundred miles west of the Missouri river and the State line, is nearly identical with that of Iowa and Missouri. The highlands are open prairies, covered with grasses; the river-bottom, a deep, rich loam, shaded by dense forests. From this first district, to about the mouth of *L' Eau qui Court* (Running Water river), it is one boundless expanse of rolling prairie, so largely intermixed with sand as to be almost unfit for ordinary agricultural purposes. The prairies are, however, carpeted with succulent grasses, affording an inexhaustible supply for herds of cattle and sheep.

"The third district is a formation of marl and earthy limestone, and extends in a belt of many miles, east and west of the Mandan village, on the most northern bend of the Missouri river, and southward across the southern boundary of the Territory. This soil can not be otherwise than very productive. I should think it especially adapted to wheat, rye, barley, and oats. I have seen, also, very fine Indian corn along the upper valleys of the Missouri river.

It is in this district that what are called *buttes* by the Canadian French, and *cerros* by the Spaniards, are profusely scattered. Here and there the traveler finds surfaces, varying in diameter from a hundred feet to a mile, elevated from fifteen to fifty feet above the surrounding surface. They are not hills or knobs, the sides of which are more or less steep and covered with grass. Their sides are nearly perpendicular, their surfaces flat, and often covered with mountain cherries and other shrubs. They have the appearance of having been suddenly elevated above the surrounding surface by some specific cause. This marl and limestone formation is, in many localities, worked into fantastic or picturesque forms, by the action of the elements. In one place, especially, called by the traders *La Mauvaise Terre* (the bad ground), and about thirty miles in diameter, it has assumed a marvelous variety of singular forms. From one point of view it assumes the aspect of an extensive and frowning fortification; from another, the appearance of an oriental city crowned with domes and minarets; and from a third, the appearance of a sterile, broken, and unattractive congregation of incongruous elements. These delusive appearances are produced by distance and the position of the sun.

"The wrecks of the diluvian period of geology are spread all over this region, and most profusely on that portion north of the Missouri river. Detached masses of rock, some of them hundreds of tons in weight, wholly unconnected with the adjacent geological formations, and evidently allied to those of the northern Rocky mountain region, dot the whole country.

"The district which I will call the fourth, lying north of

the Missouri river and west of Minesota, is a succession of undulating plains, the soil of which is quite fertile but rather dry. These plains are covered with a thick grassy sward, which sustains innumerable herds of bison, elk, and deer.

"The fifth district is at the base of the Black Hills, between that range and the Rocky mountains, and includes the valley of the Yellow Stone, of the Maria's river, and a variety of other small valleys, circumvallated by an amphitheater of mountains and gorgeous mountain scenery. The valley of the Yellow Stone is spacious, fertile, and salubrious. The streams are fringed with trees, from whence the valley expands many miles to the mountains. The traveler can almost imagine himself upon the Danube; for the valley is sprinkled over at long intervals with cyclopean structures of granite, closely assimilated in appearance, from a distant view, to the stern and solitary castles with which Europe was covered and guarded during the middle ages. But these structures exceed those of Europe in magnitude and grandeur, and the woods and waters are disposed with a taste and beauty which the highest art must ever toil after in vain. It is encircled by a rich girdle of hights and mountains, the bases and dark sides of which are obscured in shrubs, and the summits tufted with noble forest trees. And here is to be the seat of a populous and powerful community in the far future."

The writer of the foregoing is understood to be a gentleman of St. Louis, who has framed his statements partly from personal observation, and in part from the accounts of hunters and trappers who are familiar with the country described. The same writer states that snow falls at the foot of the mountains as early as in September, and in the southeastern part of the Territory, about the first of November. I had read with much interest the graphic articles of this gentleman, before starting for Kansas, and doubt not that they are, in the main, correct, though our own observations, and the opinions of others in the Territory, compel us to believe that he has underrated the extent of the fertile district which lies next west of the Missouri river, and that this district is not so abruptly terminated as he seems to suppose, but that its characteristics change gradually into those of the dry and sandy plain.

I had, also, consulted Fremont's Journal, previous to our journey, and was gratified, in passing over some of the routes he traveled, to notice the accuracy of his descriptions and observations. I should have been glad to have quoted still more largely from his valuable journal, were it not already in the hands of so many.

In Mr. Hale's book on Kansas and Nebraska, there is a quotation from a writer, not named, who made a short excursion into southeastern Nebraska, which, as affording a description of scenery, I insert here. The writer started from Council Bluffs.

"A short drive brought us to the Winter Quarters Ferry, twelve miles above on the river, where a good, well-manned and capacious steam ferry-boat was waiting, and in three minutes we landed all our company upon the far-famed soil of Nebraska. After a refreshing draught from a clear, cold spring that gushes from the hill-side, a few minutes brought us to the encampment of Messrs. Babbitt and Stiles, situated upon a pretty, grassy knoll, with the green carpet thickly bespangled with myriads of red, juicy strawberries, which, by-the-by, abound plentifully in the river-borders of this highly interesting country. A cheerful camp-fire was soon blazing, and our animals turned loose to graze.

"We encircled the broad, spread table (buffalo skins spread upon the ground), and regaled upon luxuries. At a reasonable hour the camp-fire was well replenished, and a circular bed of robes, etc., spread, and all retired in quiet to repose, and to dream of the great future of that lovely land.

"Early morn brought the report of horses being missing. A scout soon returned with the conviction that they had been stolen by the Indians. A company of horsemen started on one trail north, while we, with a small company, took the road for the Elkhorn, where we arrived (thirty miles) in good camp time, after passing over a most delightful country for nearly the whole distance. There is, however, quite a scarcity of timber, which may only be found upon the streams.

"We encamped for dinner on the Papillon, where there is some nice timber and excellent water. In approaching near the Elkhorn, a glorious and grand scenery breaks upon the vision. The eye takes in, at a glance, the country ahead for some twenty miles, giving a full view of the Elkhorn and Platte rivers, with their winding courses, groves, bluffs, and valleys; at sundown the scenery is both grand and enchanting.

"The river being high, we met with no success in fishing, although there are fine fish in the stream. Our roast venison was eaten with a relish while seated on nature's grassy carpet around the camp-fire. Here we found a number of Pawnee Indians, one of whom had a monster of a young black eagle which he had captured after having broken one of its wings. We had an excellent night's rest, and at an early hour started homeward, snatching occasionally from their native beds a cluster of sweet flowers."

The fifth division embraces the country lying at the eastern base of the Rocky mountains, and the whole of their eastern slope. The country stretching along the eastern base of the mountains has a general elevation of from four thousand to five thousand feet above the sea—it being about four thousand at the southern line of Kansas, and five thousand, around the sources of the Platte, in Nebraska. A country, thus elevated, must of course possess a cool, but healthful climate. Numerous spurs shoot out from the mountains, forming fertile valleys, with mountain-streams whose banks abound with timber, as stated by Fremont in his journal, quoted already, where he is describing the country around the sources of the Platte. Throughout this region there seems to be an abundance of pine timber, and other trees of mountain growth, and it becomes a question of great interest, whether the treasures of this immense western lumber region can be wafted eastward by being floated down the upper Missouri, the Yellow Stone, and their tributaries, the Platte, and the tributaries of the Kansas and the Arkansas.

The features of this mountain district are quite different from what many have supposed. Many probably think of the Rocky mountains as a single continuous mountain wall which the traveler mounts by a steep ascent on one side, and descends as steeply on the other. But these mountains are only the highest peaks in a vast mountainous region, varying in breadth from five hundred to nine hundred miles, and occupying a large portion of the space between the Pacific Ocean and the Mississippi river. It is an immense elevated plateau, reaching from Mexico to the farthest north, the Sierra Nevada, in California, being the westernmost high ridge, and the Rocky mountains forming the loftiest range in the east.

Over this wide space, imbosomed among the hills, are countless valleys, streams and lakes, while the mountains, up to the snow line, are covered with forests. One of these valleys, that of Salt Lake, is occupied by the Mormons. Many tribes of Indians, some of them warlike, and some at present hostile, roam over this wide country. It abounds in game of almost every variety, and it can not be doubted, that this Switzerland of the west, will yet be occupied by a bold, hardy and intelligent population. Could the Government once abandon its purposes of acquisition on the south, and foster the construction of at least three lines of railway through these regions to the Pacific, it would confer a greater benefit upon the people of the United States, than by the acquisition of every island in the West Indian seas.

The sixth district is occupied by the not well-defined sandy belt, that extends along the center of the plain, between the Missouri on the east, and the Rocky mountains, whose characteristics have been previously described, while speaking of Kansas.

West of our present line of States, and between them and

California, and the Pacific, there is an immense Territory, about equal to that occupied by the States at present, rich in agricultural and mineral resources, whose political and religious destiny depends very much upon the question, whether slavery shall be excluded from Kansas and Nebraska, and especially from the former. If Kansas is made free, the vast regions of the west and southwest will be saved from this devouring curse, which not only destroys all external prosperity, but eats out the very heart of the country. It is, apparently, the most important issue ever made in the United States, and it will never be completely met by the mere action of political parties. The determining of this question belongs of right to the churches of this land, and upon them, as the end, I think, will show, has God laid the responsibility, because it is a question of morals and religion, involving the honor of Christ.

Since writing the foregoing, I have had an opportunity of conversing with the Rev. Mr. Spencer, of the Ojibwa Mission, at St. Joseph, on the Pembina river, close on the boundary line between the United States and the British Provinces, and consequently farther north than the wide region embraced in the valley of the Yellow Stone and the upper Missouri. Mr. Spencer has just returned from the Pembina station, and having spent a winter there, his account of the climate and productions of this region is interesting, as throwing light upon the capabilities of the country lying to the southwest of his location. He informed me that a person does not suffer there from cold during the winter, more than even in the mild climate of southern Ohio; that the greater humidity of the atmosphere here, produces a sensation of cold not felt in those northern regions, at a much lower temperature. This he attributes to the dry and invigorating character of the atmosphere. Upon the whole, he considers the winters not more severe there than in Ohio, though the mercury sinks much lower. The frost commences there in September, but after the first frosts, there is usually pleasant weather for several weeks (the Indian summer), and in the latter part of October, the winter begins, when, until spring, the weather is steadily cold. Corn is not planted there till the beginning of June, but it ripens perfectly, producing fine crops. Wheat also succeeds well, as do also barley and oats; while potatoes and other roots yield large crops, and are of a very superior quality.

This tract is in the valley of the Red river of the north, and opens toward the Polar seas. As the valleys of the northern Missouri and Yellow Stone are farther south, and are sheltered by the Rocky mountains and Black Hills, the climate is, doubtless, more mild, and the whole country every way more beautiful and desirable. When it is considered, moreover, that this vast amphitheater can be reached by steamboats, it can not be doubted that it will soon be occupied by the homes of the pioneers. It can not be held much longer by Indians and wild beasts alone.

CHAPTER XXVI.

GREAT IMPORTANCE OF THE KANSAS QUESTION.

WEST of our present line of States, and between them and California, and north of the general boundary of Texas, lies a country about as large as that occupied by all the present States and the Territory of Minesota. It is a district more than one thousand miles square. Its eastern portion comprises Nebraska and Kansas, and the prairie country which lies south of Kansas, and between it and Texas. West of this, there is the broad belt of mountainous territory, reaching from Mexico to the British Provinces on the north, being from five hundred to nine hundred miles wide, and bounded westward by the Sierra Nevada, in California, and farther north by the Pacific Ocean. The Rocky mountains form the dividing line, or "ridge," between two immense water-sheds, one of which slopes eastward to the Mississippi, the other westward to the Pacific. The eastern slope has been dwelt upon in this book. The western is composed of a succession of mountains and hills, valleys and mountain basins, sparkling with lakes, and streams that flow westward toward the Pacific Ocean. This region abounds also in timber. It receives the moisture and mild influences of the western and southwestern winds from the

Pacific, which, even in Washington and Oregon render the winters short and mild. Several of the mountain peaks shoot up to the region of perpetual snow, while at their bases, as in Switzerland, are mild and beautiful valleys, and clear streams and lakes. In Mexico and New Mexico, these same mountain ranges are known to be exceedingly rich in minerals. The value of this immense Territory has not, as yet, been duly appreciated, and especially by the people of the free States. Little importance has been attached, until lately, to the whole country west of the Missouri, on the north, and of Arkansas, on the south. The great "American Desert," as it has been called, and the Rocky mountains, have, in the minds of most, probably, filled the whole space between the present States and the Pacific Ocean, excepting only California.

But it is a question not yet settled in the negative, whether this western half of the United States territory, lying beyond the Missouri and Mississippi, is not capable of supporting as large a population as that which is occupied by our present States. The beauty, fertility, and general resources of the Pacific slope of our country have doubtless been greatly underrated. The whole of this vast region is, by the Nebraska bill, virtually thrown open to slavery; for though in terms it is confined to Kansas and Nebraska, the principle of the bill is equally applicable to all our present territory, and to all which may hereafter be acquired. And this was the undoubted aim of the whole movement. It was no less a scheme than this; to gain for the slave power the control of all the unoccupied territory which we now possess, and of all which we may obtain, whether the Sandwich

Islands, Mexico, the West India islands, or Central America. The Nebraska bill was but the entering wedge to this vast iniquity. It has been said that the slaveholders care little for the possession of Kansas; that they are interested mainly in the establishment of the principle, and its future application to more valuable acquisitions. This, in one sense, may be true. They may value Cuba more than Kansas, yet it should be remembered that they are perfectly aware that the possession of Kansas is essential to the prosecution of their plan. It is the strong outwork which must, from necessity, be carried, before any other step can be taken. At the frontier of Kansas the aggressive march of the slave power is at present arrested, and as a fortress of freedom it is now invested by southern forces. It is the Crimea and Sevastopol in this western war of liberty and slavery; and far more important issues hang on the event than on the fate of the Russian fortress.

Situated as Kansas now is, it is the key of that whole great West beyond our present States. If secured for free institutions, the same causes by which it will be saved, will not only arrest the northward march of slavery, but it will also carry the dominion of freedom southward, and interpose a complete barrier to the extension of the slave power westward, and a Territory equal to the present States will thus be secured as the inheritance of freemen. Nor will the influence find its boundary here. A public sentiment, strong enough and active enough to obtain such a result, would also prevent the annexation of any territory hereafter to be placed under the curse of slavery. To secure Kansas, is to change the whole policy of the government in reference to slavery, from that of nurture and enlargement to one of discouragement and repression. Instead of marching forth to seize, on all sides, the fairest of our possessions, it would be hemmed in by the closing round it of freedom's hosts, and driven in upon itself. Left to its own unaided resources, it would be a helpless monster smitten with famine, gnashing its teeth upon itself, and perishing for lack of spoil.

On the other hand, if Kansas is won by the slave power, flushed with this victory, arrogant and unscrupulous, it will rush into fresh outrage and victory against a beaten and dispirited north, and the slaveholders will soon control directly, or indirectly, the whole Pacific slope, and the whole Mississippi valley, except its extreme northern portion, if, indeed, we may be allowed to except even that; for with the enormous political ascendency which the south would then have, she could wield and mould the north according to her will, as the past has shown in the most mortifying manner. She would add, at her pleasure, Mexico and Cuba, and gain, also, control of Central America.

All this she will be able to accomplish, if Kansas shall be won, in spite of any combination or re-construction of parties which is likely to occur. There is, as yet, no public sentiment in the north which can be relied upon, to prevent the sacrifice of the interests of freedom, when demanded by the exigency of a party. This public sentiment requires to be invigorated and made courageous, by just such a victory as the winning of Kansas would supply. Nor would this great issue be suitably met, by the mere repeal of the Nebraska bill, or the striking out of its iniquitous clause. A great opportunity of gaining for freedom perpetual ascendency in the country would then be lost. Let the fraud remain as a brand upon the southern brow, and as an everlasting memorial against the slave power. Let the north now win back its own, and then sit down on the southern frontier, freed from compromises and restrictions of all kinds, ready to go forth from this heart of the Continent, and plant its institutions on every foot of American soil. A prompt and large northern emigration would secure the whole.

CHAPTER XXVII.

A WARNING VOICE.

The impression is now widely, almost universally spread through the free States, that Kansas is already virtually won for freedom. Schemes for its salvation have been so largely discussed, that they are regarded by many as already accomplished. The plans of emigration societies have been so constantly before the public, their every movement has been so carefully noted and exulted over, that most are not aware how far the execution lags behind the promise.

Again, inasmuch as the late political triumphs have been achieved under an "Anti-Nebraska" banner, thousands suppose that through these Kansas has been secured. Then, too, an opinion is generally entertained that slaveholders themselves regard the question as one determined already against them, and that to this decision they must submit as best they may. Doubtless there are many important circumstances in the case, that favor the establishment of free institutions in Kansas. These have been already mentioned in a previous chapter. They are numerous enough to place a complete victory within the reach of the free States. If they fail, it will be from lack of sufficient interest in the subject to induce prompt and energetic action. It will be because they neglect to avail themselves of the advantages which seem to have been specially granted them in the providence of God. Against such effort as the north could easily make, and would not fail to make, if thoroughly aroused, the slave power can offer no effectual resistance. It would be compelled into quiet submission; while by the moral effect of such a triumph, every neutral mind would be inclined toward the victorious party, and anti-slavery feeling would be strengthened within the slave States themselves. There are a thousand interests and feelings already there, antagonistic to slavery, and these would show themselves in active effort, if time and circumstance should favor. The commercial interests especially, if not overawed, will ere long present in Missouri a powerful antagonism to slavery. A triumph then *may* be readily achieved—but it is not therefore, certain that it will be won.

It is at least prudent to study with care, the actual dangers which beset this cause—the real obstacles which are yet unsurmounted. In the first place, the efforts of the Emigration Societies have been met with a certain lack of enthusiasm which gives no high promise for the future, and indicates that the tone of that portion of the press, favorable to the enterprise, is yet quite in advance of the general public sentiment. Men and means have been somewhat sparingly offered to these Societies, and few from the east have as yet gone forward on their individual responsibility. The thousands which the public were led to expect, and which the slaveholders feared, have dwindled to hundreds, and the public has not been sufficiently prompt and liberal toward the Societies, to enable them to provide even for these, in an entirely satisfactory manner—according to the earnest desire of the officers and agents who have the immediate direction of affairs. For these reasons, even at the New England Settlement, the various instrumentalities, such as saw-mills, etc., could not be put in motion sufficiently early to insure the comfort of all for the winter, notwithstanding the energy and activity of the resident agents. The friends of the cause in New England should not have permitted this; nor exposed thus the Colonization enterprise to the reaction which is almost certain to come. I mention this not by way of discouragement, but that the dangers ahead may be perceived in season to avoid them. Untiring efforts should be made, not only to prevent the eastern public from sinking into indifference, but to prepare them for the future, and stir the masses with enthusiasm and hope. The plans which have been formed for the systematic settling of Kansas on a large scale, have been wisely conceived. They are adapted to the great ends in view. If successful, they will be followed by far-reaching results, which will carry down blessings to the generations to come. They ought not to be permitted to languish for the lack of effort, or sympathy, or money, or men. Taking it all in all, this is the largest idea now before the American mind.

Again, the political movement which, under an Anti-Nebraska flag has just swept the country, can not be safely relied upon for the salvation of Kansas. It is questionable, to say the least, whether its leading sentiment will be one opposed to slavery—when it has assumed the form and compactness of a party. Political parties have hitherto used the anti-slavery feeling of the country very much as a vessel uses a steam-tug, when becalmed, or to get it well out of harbor, and then it spreads its sails and commits itself to other influences. The steam-tug should be converted into an ocean steamer that can make a voyage on its own account.

The political party which is now likely to become the dominant one, has quite other purposes lying nearer to its heart than the abolition, or even repression of slavery. If to secure these purposes, some anti-slavery work is *necessary*, it may be done, if not, Kansas will be forgotten, or the iniquity even be consummated. The sooner the people cease to cheat themselves with the idea that in these shoutings over political victories they hear deliverance for Kansas, the better. It may, or it may not be so, according as party exigencies shall demand. Let those who desire to plant free institutions in Kansas beware of leaning upon that which may break and pierce them. Moreover, the slaveholders are neither disheartened, as yet, nor indifferent nor inactive. They are more hopeful now than when we were in the Territory. They are gathering assurance and determination. They see the magnitude of the issue; and a Missourian has lately expressed the opinion that to prevent Kansas from becoming a free State, Missouri should pour half her population, "*temporarily, at least,*" into the Territory. This language, however extravagant, is not to be regarded as having no significance. It means that Missouri shall supply voters enough from her own soil to meet the question when it arises, and that they will force their way to the ballot-box with pistols and the bowie-knife. A fit illustration is offered, by an expedition fitted out a few days since, as I was informed by one then on the spot, at Weston,

Missouri, to control the election of delegates to Congress in the Territory.

A convention of *Missourians* held a convention in *Missouri*, for the nomination of a delegate for Kansas, and then a body of about three hundred armed men, went over into the Territory on the day appointed to enforce *their nomination* made on the other side of the river by residents in Missouri. They intend to overawe the settlers, by demanding a vote for every fictitious claim which their tools or accomplices have registered; and they openly declare, that if those who have made these claims can not vote, though residing in Missouri, that all others shall be prevented by force and arms. Doubtless they would, and will do these things, and worse, if they dare; and they will dare, if the number of anti-slavery settlers is small. Had the eastern emigration, however, even approached its early promise, these proceedings would never have been heard of. Hence, inasmuch as the territorial legislature is not to be convened, as is said, until next spring or summer, the immense importance of continuous efforts, during the winter, to secure a large and early emigration in the spring. By this means the whole question would be promptly met and settled, and the storms and bluster on the frontier would subside into a calm, and these threats would be heard of no more. The friends of human freedom through the north, then, should be made to understand that there is great and real danger in regard to Kansas, and that success will require earnest work; and yet success is, under God, perfectly certain, if their work is well and promptly done.

These violent counsels and measures are the work of a

small minority of the people of Missouri, but left to themselves, they may control the action of the State and the destiny of Kansas. It is said that there is a secret organization rapidly extending itself, whose sole purpose is to secure Kansas for slavery, by numbers, fraud, or force. If this is so, it will receive the earnest co-operation of the prominent leaders among slaveholders, and of hundreds of traitors to freedom in the free States also. It remains to be seen, whether the freemen of the north will suffer this robbery of their rightful patrimony to be thus perpetuated.

The foregoing information, in regard to a "secret society," we received from a gentleman of our acquaintance who has just returned from Kansas (November 28th), and since that period we have found in a St. Louis paper the following confirmation, by which it will be seen that a United States Senator is at the head of this new scheme of iniquity. By such proceedings let the north be warned, and also aroused:—

"Senator Atchison is at present engaged in the upper country, *organizing a secret society, to consist of five thousand persons, pledged to repair into Kansas, on the day of the first election held there, to vote slavery into that Territory.* Of this we have authentic information, and in a few days we shall expose the whole scheme; for while we wish to see the people of Kansas determine the question of their own domestic institutions, we can not and will not tolerate such an unlawful and iniquitous rascality as that of 'Drunken Davy's,' which proposes that a large body of men who are not, and do not intend to become residents of that Territory, shall, by force and violence, override the sense and wishes of its legitimate settlers."

CHAPTER XXVIII.

CHRISTIAN OBLIGATION—CHRISTIAN COLONIZATION.

In considering the magnitude of the interests which are at stake—the extent and value of the region to be lost or won for freedom—by the action of this generation, the question ought to present itself to every mind, What can I do; what ought I to do; how can Kansas, Nebraska, and that great adjoining West, be most effectually secured? Especially should every Christian make this a subject of prayerful inquiry. A great practical question is here presented to the Church, and especially to that portion of it that professes a deep anxiety for the removal of slavery, or even a desire to confine it within its present limits. Will the friends of freedom be justified in leaving the settlement of Kansas to the operation of the common causes which have governed emigration elsewhere, or are they called upon, in the emergency which has suddenly arisen, to improve, by unusual measures, the opportunity which has been presented in the providence of God? It is questionable whether the opponents of the slave power have, in general, viewed this Nebraska fraud in its proper light. It has been regarded by most as a signal victory, achieved by the south over northern interests and rights. If, however, the friends of human rights are now true to God and their cause, it will be seen that the south has smitten her own interests with a fatal blow. The Missouri compromise was slavery's northern wall of defense. For although there was no express stipulation, that free institutions should not cross the line agreed upon, there was an understood moral obligation, the force of an implied compact, which would have arrested, during its continuance, the progress of freedom at that bound. Should we not be encouraged, when the south, in its folly, has, with her own hands, and against all remonstrance, torn this compact in pieces, and exposed herself and her institutions in an open field? Ought we not to discern in this the favoring providence of God, which thus offers to free institutions an unlooked-for opportunity, and opens before them an unexpected field? For if slavery may now march northward, if it has tho power, the whole south is, in like manner, thrown open to freedom. Let us suppose that the Missouri compromise shall stand perpetually repealed, and the struggle is to go forward without territorial restrictions on either side; and add one other supposition, that the north is true to herself, and with the comparative progress of the north and the south as our guide, who can doubt as to the ultimate result? Instead of mourning that the north has been opened to slavery, let us rejoice that all restrictions upon the progress of liberty are taken away, and that there is not a foot of soil now on our continent, where she may not set up her banner and plant her institutions. If northern freemen were fully awake, and prepared for the performance of their whole duty, this would be the appropriate feeling;

and instead of aggressions upon northern territory by slavery, we should hear of the march of free institutions toward the Gulf.

The best method of winning back this stolen inheritance of the north, will perhaps appear, if we bestow a moment's attention upon the different methods of emigration now followed or proposed. The discomforts and perils, the disadvantages of all kinds attending the common manner of settling a new region are so great, and so manifest, that it is surprising that it has not, ere this, been systematically undertaken, when the superior advantages of Colonies are perfectly obvious. Too often the settler is for years cut off from all the benefits and comforts of civilized life; from religious privileges; from schools, society, and markets. The older portions of the household drag out often a sickly and sad existence, shut out from most of those little luxuries and enjoyments which once rendered life joyous; while the children grow up without education or culture of any kind, rude proprietors, at last, of valuable tracts of land, where, perhaps, the third generation may be educated.

Pioneer life, while producing such magnificent general results, has caused suffering, and sickness, and death, in thousands of individual homes, and entailed semi-barbarism upon a portion of the survivors. But all, or most of these evils may be easily avoided by the formation of Colonies—and especially now, when so large a portion of the best of our public lands may be reached, cheaply and quickly, by steamboats and railways. It is not now an impracticable thing to transplant a whole community, with all its various members and occupations, so that nearly all the comforts and benefits of an old society may be at once enjoyed in the new position. Churches, schools, professional men, merchants and mechanics of all kinds, may locate themselves together, and commence the new life with all the operations and relations of the old. The Christian will be connected at once with the church and its ordinances, nor become, as so many thousands of pioneers have, a lost sheep in the wilderness, or left to bring scandal upon religion. The individual will not be isolated and lost, nor will his influence be neutralized or his principles endangered by the power of strange associations. He will not be thrown among strangers. It will be a community either of old friends and neighbors, or a company drawn together by common aims and affinities; and thus supported by each other, a small band, instead of losing, as so many individual pioneers have done, their original characteristics and former good practices, will send an influence outward, and stamp their image upon others.

Every such homogeneous colony becomes a center of life, and source of power. In no country ever opened to the settler, could all this be more easily accomplished than in Kansas and portions of Nebraska—but especially in Kansas. Seven or eight days of easy travel by railways and steamboats, will suffice to transport a colony even from Massachusetts to this land; and then next spring, the valley of the Kansas can be ascended by steamboat to Fort Riley, (about one hundred and seventy-five miles), by the river. In this short period, or a little more, a colony from almost any point in the northern States can be located on some of the most fertile lands of earth, where the fields are perfectly prepared for the plow, and for the reception of any crop. and where natural meadows and pastures stretch away on every side, to furnish hay and grass for any amount of stock. If then, these colonists possess some ready money—and without means men can not be comfortable anywhere—what can prevent them from surrounding themselves, in a single season, with most of the comforts of an eastern home, while even the *immediate* future would open with richer promise than ever before. To pioneer life, such as it has formerly been, especially in timber countries—such as it presents itself to most minds that have heard tales of frontier hardship and suffering—colonization in such a country as Kansas, bears not the remotest resemblance. Every man among the thousands that yearly build houses on new sites, and lay out new grounds, does what is required of the settler of Kansas. He locates upon a tract of land all ready for any purpose, and then lays out his grounds, and erects his dwelling. With such a colony, the whole machinery of society would at once go on as usual, and each would find himself in the midst of old neighbors and friends, or among new associates, of a spirit similar to his own, and surrounded by the conveniences of older society — while life, as in all new settlements, would have a larger and more genial development. The site of such a colony would at once become a business center for the surrounding region, and the value of lands would be rapidly increased. To these general advantages of colonization, the Emigration Societies propose to add the aid of capital and associated influence, by which cheap fares can be obtained for emigrants, along the lines of travel, and to erect mills, and aid in all suitable ways, in the establishment of a town, where numbers may at once be collected in an organized society. They expect to be remunerated for capital expended, by the increased value of the lands, which the Company itself retains. These advantages may all be secured by private association in a single colony.

But the highest possible exhibition of this scheme, and by far the most effectual for the salvation of Kansas, would be colonization by bands of Christians—"Christian colonization." Such a movement need not be isolated or exclusive in its character or aims. Certainly, there would be nothing objectionable, if Christians should agree to act as such, and in organized capacity, in connection with the efforts of others, for the purpose of establishing the Gospel and freedom on the soil of Kansas. Nothing is more obvious, than if Emigrant Churches could be organized in sufficient numbers, and planted in that Territory, so that they should become the nuclei around which society there would form itself, that Kansas, with God's blessing, would not only be a free State, but a model State. If the Christians who may make Kansas their home, instead of being scattered abroad, could be settled in communities, from the first, and bound to each other by Christian sympathies, neighborhood attachments, and the ties of Church relationship, what a waste of influence would be prevented! what a power would be created at these Christian centers, whose silent influence would flow forth, shaping and blessing all things! This presents itself in the light of a missionary effort on the large scale, and in the most effective form. If Churches could thus be formed at different points in our land, either connected with colonies or forming a colony by themselves, to become in Kansas the germs of towns and cities, and to plant the seeds of all right things around them, how incalculable a benefit would thus be conferred upon Kansas, and how far into the future the movement would reach, in its influence upon slavery and the destinies of that remote west, even to the Pacific! How cheaply this operation might be performed! Every godly man or woman thus settling there, would be a missionary of the most effective kind, and once there, a man would not only sustain himself, but would be adding to the general wealth of the country, while laying the foundations of the kingdom of Christ. Why might not such Churches be organized in different parts of the country, and the different missionary societies aid them in sustaining their pastors? and why should not the same large-hearted benevolence, which sends yearly hundreds of thousands of dollars into foreign lands, contribute with more zeal and liberality still, to such a cause, so intimately connected with the progress of Christ's cause at home, and the interests of the country at large? It presents, too, a noble opportunity to lay aside denominational feelings, and unite in a common work for God. If at any locality there are Christians of different sects, who wish to emigrate to Kansas, why should they not unite in an organization liberal enough to embrace all evangelical Christians, and then go forth together, not to establish a sectarian religion, but to save, by their joint efforts, Kansas from slavery, and lay the broad foundations of the Gospel under the society forming there? Such an experiment might afford the opportunity for the exhibition of a higher and nobler form of Christianity than now exists in the country. Separated from old associations—old barriers thrown down—theological differences laid aside and forgotten, and drawn together by the power of new and interesting relations, and in circumstances more favorable for the cultivation of the affections—the idea of Christian brotherhood might thus, perhaps, be more nearly realized than it can be under the more rigid forms of older communities, and Churches more nearly conformed to primitive models and primitive character, might manifest the power of a fresher and more spiritual life.

If Kansas and Nebraska could be occupied by such Churches, composed of men who, while laboring to shut out slavery from the Territory, would not forget to exclude it also from church fellowship and communion, and would, moreover, see that a sound Christian literature were circulated in the families and communities about them—a literature not in alliance with popular and powerful sin—a work would thereby be done, by which the whole country might ultimately be saved from slavery, and over which men and angels might rejoice together!

THE END.

www.ingramcontent.com/pod-product-compliance
Lightning Source LLC
LaVergne TN
LVHW050528100826
845148LV00002B/473

* 9 7 8 1 4 2 5 5 1 9 3 1 5 *